Guardians of creation

Nature in theology and the Christian life

Lawrence Osborn

APOLLOS (an imprint of Inter-Varsity Press)
38 De Montfort Street, Leicester LE1 7GP, England

First published 1993

British Library Cataloguing in Publication Data
A catalogue record for this book is available from the British Library.

ISBN 0–85110–951–9

Photoset by Parker Typesetting Service, Leicester
Printed in England by Clays Ltd, St Ives plc

Contents

Acknowledgments

I wish to thank Latimer House, Oxford, for permission to make extensive use of my Latimer Study, *Stewards of Creation: Environmentalism in the Light of Biblical Teaching* (Latimer Study No. 34, 1990) in the preparation of the present work.

Foreword

During the first two weeks of June 1992, the largest international conference ever held – the United Nations Conference on Environment and Development – was staged in Rio de Janeiro. Well over one hundred heads of government attended. Green movements and pressure groups held a wide variety of associated meetings. The media were present in unprecedented numbers; the prelude to the conference and the conference itself were widely reported world-wide.

A number of factors during the 1980s have led to the generation of the enormous interest in the environment which led up to the Rio Conference. First, nations in both the developed and the developing world have experienced a series of environmental crises. An accident at the Chernobyl nuclear power station in Russia affected to a greater or lesser extent most countries in Western Europe. Major droughts have very seriously affected various parts of Africa; areas of Bangladesh and China have been devastated by floods; there is a continuing threat as deserts expand irretrievably. Secondly, scientists have become much more aware of the potential damage to the environment of human activities. The discovery of the ozone hole over Antarctica resulting from the growth in the use of chlorofluorocarbons (CFCs) in refrigerators and aerosol sprays is a telling example of how the environment can be affected in unexpected ways. Through the work of the Intergovernmental Panel on Climate Change, the Scientific Assessment for which I have been privileged to chair, the influence of the burning of fossil fuels leading to global warming and climate change has become better understood and more widely known. Thirdly, public awareness of environmental issues has grown enormously through the influence of Green parties and pressure groups and through the increasing attention of the media.

Two international treaties were up for signature in Rio, one a Climate Convention dealing with global climate change, the other one on biodiversity concerned with the loss of species as areas of tropical forest and other natural habitats are lost. Both of these treaties concern global problems of concern to all nations whatever their state of development. Both treaties also recognize that the actions of one nation can have environmental impact affecting all nations.

The discussions concerning these treaties expose two of the major problems surrounding the organization of international action on environmental issues. The first is concerned with what is the appropriate response and action in an area such as that of climate change where there remains substantial scientific uncertainty. How can questions of environmental risk be incorporated in policies based, for instance, on the principle of sustainable development? The second problem is that of the ownership of technical knowhow and the difficulty of attaining useful transfer of technology from the developed to the developing world, which in turn raises the whole question of where the resources are to come from to combat environmental degradation especially in developing countries.

Because environmental problems are large and pressing, all of us are forced to think about our attitudes to the environment. Some believe that whatever the problems, appropriate technical fixes will be found so that we need not be too concerned. Others feel the immensity of the problems of today (in the poverty stricken parts of the Third World it must be very difficult to feel otherwise) and are prepared to shelve the problems of tomorrow. Some want to go back to 'nature' and find a simple lifestyle not recognizing that by so doing they are essentially opting out of the global problems we face. Yet others believe very strongly in the value of the natural world and the importance of preserving it at all costs. Then there is the question as to our responsibility to future generations, to which a variety of answers are commonly given.

The Green movements give various answers to these questions, sometimes backing them up by reference to religious attitudes, especially ones culled from Eastern religions. But where in the debate have been the Christians? What has the church to say on environmental issues? Some have blamed the Protestant ethic for leading to over-exploitation of the environment. Is this a fair accusation?

Although many Christians go along broadly with environmental concern, very few have given serious thought to the issues involved. Some, particularly amongst evangelicals, deliberately ignore the environment as being, they believe, only of subsidiary importance to more spiritual matters.

As Lawrence Osborn points out in this book such an attitude is not true to the message of the Bible nor is it true to much of Christian tradition throughout the centuries. What is urgently required is a thoroughgoing theology of the environment which can guide Christian thought and response to environmental concerns. Dr Osborn, having experience in both science and theology, is well qualified to provide such a basis and I commend the effective and practical way he has woven the environmental science and the theology together.

William Temple wrote in the 1930s 'It may be safely said that one ground for the hope of Christianity that may make good its claim to be the one true faith lies in the fact that it is the most avowedly materialistic of all the great religions ... Its own most central saying is "The Word was made flesh" ... By the very nature of its central doctrine Christianity is committed to a belief ... in the reality of matter and its place in the divine scheme.' To demonstrate the relevance of Christianity for the twenty-first century, we need to apply the great doctrines of creation and incarnation to our growing environmental concerns. Lawrence Osborn's book provides us with a good start.

John Houghton
August 1992

CHAPTER ONE

The environmental crisis: an introductory update

In Köhln, a town of monks and bones,
And pavements fang'd with murderous stones
And rags, and hags, and hideous wenches;
I counted two and seventy stenches,
All well defined and several stinks!
Ye Nymphs that reign o'er sewers and sinks,
The river Rhine, it is well known,
Doth wash your city of Cologne;
But tell me, Nymphs, what power divine
Shall henceforth wash the river Rhine?
(Samuel Taylor Coleridge)

As that little poem makes clear, concern about our effect on the environment is by no means unique to the twentieth century. Indeed, two centuries before Coleridge, the diarist John Evelyn was already campaigning vigorously against atmospheric pollution and deforestation.

This century, however, has seen a dramatic heightening of environmental anxiety. Much of this anxiety, like that of Coleridge and Evelyn, is inspired by concern about the human cost of environmental degradation. But many people today are also concerned about our impact on nature in itself.

As we embark on the last decade of the twentieth century such concerns are likely to take on a new urgency. *Glasnost* and *perestroika*, the dismantling of the Berlin Wall and the promise of deep cuts in the developed world's nuclear and conventional arsenals have given us sudden relief from the threat of an apocalyptic global war. But I suspect our nuclear anxieties will be replaced by ever-more pressing environmental anxieties.

Thus Christianity today cannot afford to ignore the natural environment. At both theoretical and practical levels, Christians urgently need to develop a Christian environmental ethic. And that ethic needs to be undergirded by fundamental theological attention to the environment as a dimension of God's good creation. The aim of this book is to re-examine the disparate and often inconsistent Christian responses to contemporary environmentalism and to propose a possible line of development as a basis for further theological debate, prayer and practical Christian action.

But first, by way of introduction, we should ask what in particular is the basis for present environmental fears and what has led to the recent explosion in environmental awareness.

1. The ecological perspective

Arguably, current environmental fears owe their influence in large measure to their perceived scientific basis. Central to this scientific basis is the relatively young science of ecology.

The term 'ecology' was coined last century by the German biologist Ernst Haeckel, to describe the study of the relationship between living organisms and their environment. In doing so he was following up hints contained in Darwin's classic, *The Origin of Species*, that such a study could yield fruitful insights.

Fundamental to this science is the concept of an *ecosystem*. This may be defined as an interacting system of plants, animals and micro-organisms together with their physical environment. Clearly such a concept presents the biologists who use it with major practical difficulties. For example, how can we ever be certain that we have identified all the living and non-living components of a particular ecosystem? However, in spite of such difficulties, it is possible to identify and study a wide range of fairly well-defined ecosystems.

Contrary to popular belief, such studies are not concerned primarily with such matters as the effect of pollution or other human activities. The science of ecology is fundamentally an attempt to understand the dynamics of ecosystems in themselves. Why is a given species of animal or plant present in these numbers? How do population numbers change over time, if at all? What are the biological and physical factors which govern these levels? Originally, at least, the issue of human impact on natural ecosystems was of secondary importance.

For our purposes the most important feature of the science of ecology is its fundamental assumption about the natural world. The ecological view is that the living creatures in any given environment are interdependent and have to be understood as a whole. Arthur Peacocke offers the following description of the ecological approach to life:

> All plants and animals live in complex systems consisting of many crossflows and exchanges of energy and matter in various chemical forms of such baffling complexity that only the advent of computers, and the development of systems theory, have given any hope of analysing them.[1]

This contrasts sharply with the reductionism of classical physics which seeks understanding by breaking a system down into its component parts and treating them in isolation from the whole. By contrast, ecology is a science concerned with the dynamics of extremely complex systems.

The complexity of ecosystems is further compounded by the fact that ecosystems are themselves interdependent. There are no clearly defined boundaries between ecosystems and it has become increasingly clear that this is true even of ecosystems which are separated by thousands of

[1]Peacocke, 1979, p. 258.

miles.[1] As a consequence there has been an increasing tendency to think in terms of a global ecosystem (in spite of doubts about the scientific value of such an all-embracing concept).

One of the most forceful advocates of this view is undoubtedly James Lovelock. He argues that the global ecosystem should be regarded as an entity (or even an organism) in its own right: an entity which he has named 'Gaia'. His working definition of Gaia is as follows:

> a complex entity involving the Earth's biosphere, atmosphere, oceans, and soil; the totality constituting a feedback or cybernetic system which seeks an optimal physical and chemical environment for life on this planet.[2]

This interdependence is an important factor in the stability of the global ecosystem. In fact, Lovelock uses it to explain the stability of the earth's climate over a period of approximately three-thousand-million years. This relative stability is remarkable because over the same period there has been a thirty percent increase in the sun's energy. Central to his hypothesis is the assumption that the earth's ecosystems interlock to create a global network of negative feedback systems.

Negative feedback is a concept well known in the world of engineering. It refers to situations in which a change in one part of a system causes other parts to react so that balance is restored. The classical example is the governor which regulates the pressure in a steam engine. Another example is that of the thermostat in a central-heating system. In the case of Gaia, Lovelock postulates systems which not only maintain the planet's climate but also regulate such things as atmospheric composition and the chemical composition of sea water, and limit the impact of individual species on the environment as a whole.

Two further factors contributing to the stability of an ecosystem may be picked out as being particularly susceptible

[1] For example, one effect of deforestation in the Himalayas has been a serious increase in the flooding of lowland Bangladesh.

[2] Lovelock, 1979, p. 11.

to human influence. These are the sheer amount of biological material in the system and its diversity. A simple illustration of this is the fact, well known to naturalists, that it is easier to maintain a stable ecosystem in a large aquarium than in a goldfish bowl.

Just why bigger ecosystems are more stable is not fully understood. The role of diversity is easier to explain. For example, an ecosystem containing several species of scavenger which thrive best in slightly different conditions is less likely to suffer the loss of all its scavengers as a result of some climatic change. Biological diversity does for an ecosystem what redundancy does for a spacecraft guidance system (a network of three computers working in parallel is less likely to fail than a single computer).

This talk of stability, however, should not be taken to mean that natural ecosystems are unchanging. They are stable, but their stability is dynamic rather than static. Freak weather conditions or outbreaks of disease may decimate particular species within an ecosystem, but this is likely to affect the system in such a way as to compensate for their loss. Conversely, a mild winter may cause an aphid population explosion. As a result there is likely to be a corresponding population explosion amongst their natural predators (*e.g.* ladybirds) which will restore the balance. Nor is such change confined to local variations within a larger, essentially static system. On the contrary, many ecosystems change naturally. For example, the gradual silting-up of a pond leads to a progression through marshland and grassland to a stable ecosystem (or 'climax' as ecologists call it), usually forest or tundra depending on the climate.

2. From ecology to environmentalism

For the sake of clarity it is important to draw a distinction between ecology and environmentalism. The former is an academic discipline and, as befits an academic discipline, may at times seem to have little to do with the world of Chernobyl, Seveso and toxic waste dumps.

Environmentalism is a popular response to the perceived threat to the natural environment. It is an increasingly important aspect of popular culture rather than an academic discipline. It follows that relatively few of those who are active in the environmentalist movement will be trained ecologists in the academic sense (though many may have a good lay grounding in the subject).

In order to get a clearer perspective on environmentalism as distinct from ecology we must turn to the issue of the kind of crisis we are facing.

3. The contours of environmental concern

Like all other living creatures, human beings tend to modify the environment in their own favour. However, our combination of intelligence and social organization has resulted in an unprecedented impact on the environment. With humankind this tendency to modify the environment has ceased to be instinctive. Instead, individuals and societies may choose between a variety of environment-modifying strategies out of boredom, desire for pleasure, for self-aggrandizement, for national glory, or for the good of humanity, posterity, or nature.

It is impossible to list all the ways in which we influence the environment. However, four major areas of human activity are generally regarded as harmful to natural ecosystems: the destruction of ecosystems, pollution, population growth and resource depletion (the last two being closely related in most of the literature). These areas also map out the changing focus of environmental concern over the past four decades.

a. Destruction of ecosystems

Animal lovers have for many years been concerned with the preservation of rare species. Thus many of the earliest environmentalist pressure groups were set up to protect animals, plants and places of natural beauty. Over the years, growing public awareness of ecology has shifted the emphasis from treating rare species in isolation (*e.g.* breeding programmes in captivity) to the habitats in which they live (*e.g.* campaigns to save the rainforests). Very often the reason a species is endangered is not direct hunting by man but rather the destruction of the environment in which it thrives.

The destruction of complex forest ecosystems to make way for fresh farmland (or urban environments) strikes at the very heart of ecological stability. We are currently tearing down the tropical forests at a rate which can be measured in acres per second! This is particularly worrying since, although these forests cover only 7% of the earth's surface, they are home to well over 50% of the planet's animal and plant species. Recent estimates suggest that, as a result of our activities, species are becoming extinct at a rate of about one hundred per day (one thousand times the estimated rate of extinction prior to the Industrial Revolution). What we are doing is replacing the very complex ecosystems which form the backbone of the earth's capacity to regulate its climate, atmosphere and so on, with much simpler and, hence, less stable ecosystems. Ten years ago James Lovelock issued the following warning about the potential effects of increasing exploitation of the tropics: 'Here man may sap the vitality of Gaia by reducing productivity and by deleting key species in her life-support system.'[1]

In this move towards simpler ecosystems there is a point of no return beyond which the system is no longer capable of regulating itself. Many agricultural ecosystems are like this. They can be maintained only by human intervention: artificial fertilizers, chemical pesticides and irrigation. The fear now haunting environmentalists is that our destruction of natural habitats is approaching the point at which vital functions of the global ecosystem will be damaged beyond repair.

b. Pollution

Towards the end of the 1950s attention began to be focused on less obvious forms of human impact on the environment. In particular, people began to be concerned about the effects of industrial and agricultural pollution. Many of the present generation of environmental activists were introduced to the ecological dangers of pollution by Rachel Carson's environmental classic, *Silent Spring*. Since its publication in 1962, pollution has replaced the direct destruction of habitats as the most feared way in which we affect our environment.

Pollution of the natural environment takes many forms:

[1]Lovelock, 1979, p. 121.

domestic refuse and sewage, agricultural pollution (waste from intensive farming, insecticides in the food chain, fertilizer in water supplies) and industrial waste (slag heaps, toxic chemicals, and so on). But none has captured public attention more than atmospheric pollution. The 1980s may well go down as the decade in which we became conscious of the extent to which we are poisoning the very air we breathe. It was the decade in which we became aware of acid rain, the thinning of the earth's ozone layer and global warming due to the emission of so-called *greenhouse gases*. And, as if to confirm that judgment, two of the most serious environmental accidents of the last decade involved atmospheric pollution: toxic gas in Bhopal and radioactive fallout from Chernobyl. The most serious environmental crime of recent years has also been a case of atmospheric pollution: the burning of Kuwait's oil wells.

Acid rain has been observed in Canada and many European countries. It is thought to be responsible for serious widespread damage to forests and woodlands as well as increasing the acidity of lakes and rivers, making them less hospitable to fish. The immediate cause is rain water washing acidic gases out of the atmosphere. Many environmentalists point to the vast quantity of such gases produced by the burning of fossil fuels in industrialized countries as the obvious culprit. But, as with most environmental problems, the explanation is not that simple. Recent scientific studies have suggested that oceanic algae is a major emitter of these gases (particularly dimethyl sulphide). Why then has acid rain only become a problem in recent decades? One suggestion is that the additional burden of acidic gases in industrial regions forces rapid dumping of these acids into rainfall where sea air meets polluted air. Thus, instead of being harmlessly dissipated over large areas, it is concentrated with destructive effect.[1]

Another effect of atmospheric pollution, and one which seems to have particular symbolic significance for modern western society, is the *thinning of the ozone layer*. Ozone is an unstable chemical consisting of three oxygen atoms. At ground level it exists only in trace quantities (which is fortunate since it is extremely poisonous!). However, it occurs

[1] Lovelock, 1988, pp. 159–163.

freely in a layer of the atmosphere about twenty-five kilometres above the earth's surface. Here it forms a very effective filter against the sun's ultraviolet radiation. The loss of this layer could lead to a significant global increase in the incidence of skin cancer.

The cause for concern is the widespread domestic and industrial use of a family of gases called *chlorofluorocarbons* (or CFCs). These gases are non-toxic and, under normal conditions, very stable. Thus they were regarded as ideal aerosol propellants and refrigerants. Unfortunately, they are also very efficient at mopping up free ozone. When it was first pointed out that they could pose a threat to the ozone layer, the suggestion was widely dismissed as the stuff of science fiction. However, the discovery of a hole in the ozone layer over Antarctica (more precisely a region in which the ozone levels are abnormally low) has turned this piece of science fiction into a frightening possibility.

A third form of atmospheric pollution which is currently of great concern is the emission of *greenhouse gases*. The best known of these is carbon dioxide (a major by-product of all burning of fossil fuels). As a family they get their name from the fact that they increase the atmosphere's capacity to retain heat (rather like the glass in a greenhouse). Without them the earth's mean temperature could be as low as about −20°C. Since the advent of the Industrial Revolution the human race has been steadily adding to the atmospheric stock of greenhouse gases, with the result that mean temperatures have been increasing gradually. It is estimated that if steps are not taken to control such emissions, the planet's temperature could rise by as much as 4°C in the next century. The predicted effects of this rise include a global rise in sea levels and dramatic changes in global weather patterns. But, quite apart from the climatic effects, increased carbon dioxide levels could have a damaging effect on many of the world's major food crops.

c. Population growth and resource depletion

The early 1970s saw environmental concern shift to some extent from pollution to the issues of a rapidly increasing world population and the ever-increasing demands for raw materials. This new emphasis was encapsulated in two documents: *A Blueprint for Survival* and *The Limits to Growth.* Although the revival of economic liberalism in the late 1970s and early 1980s brought with it a more optimistic view of our capacity to cope with these problems, they have quite recently come to the fore once again. Thus an article in *Time* could comment that, 'Ultimately, no problem may be more threatening to the earth's environment than the proliferation of the human species.'[1]

Strictly speaking, these issues are problems of a different order to those of pollution and direct environmental destruction. They are part of the cause of those other problems. However, we must tread warily here. Population pressure can easily be exploited by people in developed countries as a strategy for shifting blame from themselves to poorer nations. Some right-wing environmentalists use it as an argument for withholding aid from the Third World. They advocate a brutal 'life-boat ethic'[2] which envisages permitting famine and disease to rage unchecked in order to increase the developed world's prospects for survival.

Population pressure *is* part of the problem. However, it is an extremely complex issue and should certainly not be used as a pretext for evading our own environmental responsibility.

4. The nature of the crisis

The environmental crisis is not primarily a technological problem. That is to say, while technology has been partly to blame for the present situation, we cannot look to it as our saviour. At best technology may help to alleviate some of the symptoms of the crisis. A technological 'fix' for the environmental crisis is not realistic and, if it were, one might still question its desirability. Do we really want to make the image of a 'Spaceship Earth' a reality? Many environmentalists would agree with the comment that 'the metaphor is, in fact, ecologically terrifying. A spaceship is completely a human

[1]*Time*, 2 January, 1989, p. 33.
[2]This approach to ethics is often associated with the work of Garrett Hardin (*e.g.* Hardin, 1972).

artifact, designed to sustain human life and for no other purpose.'[1]

Nor is the environmental crisis a problem of the environment in the sense that it is not merely one more natural challenge for the human race to face and overcome. Before we can begin to seek appropriate solutions we must recognize the unpalatable fact that the crisis is largely of our own making. It is a *human* problem.

However, before looking more closely at the environmental crisis as a human problem, I want to qualify my use of the term 'crisis'. There are certain things commonly associated with the term which I do not wish to imply when I use it in this context.

To speak of it as a crisis can give the false impression that the present situation came about suddenly and unforeseeably. It may encourage us to overlook the gradual accumulation of contributory factors over a period of many centuries. This in turn misleads us into focusing exclusively upon the technological contribution to the environmental problem (and, as we shall see, this has important implications for attempts to trace a philosophical or spiritual root for the present 'crisis'). At the same time it offers us another strategy for blame avoidance: if we could not foresee it, we cannot be held responsible. Both of these effects lead to a limiting of the possible responses.

It may also tempt us to see the present as standing in a unique relationship to both past and future. This is likely to have two major effects on analyses of our relationship to the environment.

First, it presents our problems as somehow more serious than at any previous period (the more extreme expressions suggesting that the problem is qualitatively different from that facing earlier generations). This can result in a particular historical (or prehistorical) epoch being idolized as a golden age.

Second, it suggests that decisions taken now may radically affect the future. Positively, this does tend to restore the responsibility evaded by arguing that the crisis was unforeseeable. Our forefathers may not have been to blame for the

[1] L. White, 1973, p. 63.

legacy they bequeathed to us, but we can see what they could not. Therefore, we bear the responsibility for making decisions which will affect the lives of all future generations. The negative side of this unique relationship to the future is that 'crisis' suggests a brief transition period before we achieve a new stable state. Our decisions take on a life or death quality. If we decide wrongly, it is suggested, there will be no future generations. Conversely, many environmentalists seem to imply that if we make the right decisions we can look forward to a golden age: a restoration of Arcadia (or Eden).

5. The roots of the environmental crisis

Can we pursue the search for roots beyond the immediate agricultural, technological and economic causes of the problems outlined above? The western intellectual tradition with its insistence that thought (in the broadest sense) comes before action, would certainly encourage us to do so. And, since most environmentalists have been brought up in that tradition, it is not surprising to find them seeking the roots of the environmental crisis beyond the immediately visible aspects of human behaviour in the realms of our beliefs and attitudes. The philosopher William Blackstone offers the following summary of the attitudes and values widely held to be responsible for the present situation:

> The basic underlying causes . . . are mistaken values and attitudes – the attitudes that we can exploit the environment without restrictions, that the production of goods is more important than the people who use them, that nature will provide unlimited resources, that we have no obligation to future generations to conserve resources, that continued increases in human population is desirable and that the right to have as many children as one wants is an inviolable right, that the answer to the problems of technology is more technology, and that gross differences and inequities in the distribution of

goods and services are quite acceptable.[1]

In general, three widely held beliefs are regarded as significant causal factors underlying the present situation: the right to exploit nature (whether to benefit humankind as a whole, a particular nation, or social class, or corporate grouping, or an individual); the acceptance (or positive approval) of population growth; and, belief in the progress of human society towards a specific (but variously defined) goal. To this list is sometimes added a concern for posterity.

6. Conclusion

In this brief overview of the environmental crisis, I have attempted to shift the emphasis from particular problems and immediate solutions to what many environmentalists regard as the underlying cause, namely, western attitudes to the environment. But how did the attitudes cited here evolve? It is often suggested that the Judaeo-Christian tradition has been an important factor and it is to such accusations that we shall turn in the next chapter.

[1]Blackstone, 1974, p. 16.

CHAPTER TWO
The culpability of Christianity?

From the insistence that the crisis has its roots in the attitudes and values of western society it is but a short step to seeing it as a spiritual crisis. Since the Judaeo-Christian traditions have played a formative role in our society, it is not surprising to find widespread criticism of them in environmentalist literature. In *Time* Magazine's recent survey of environmental problems it was asserted that,

> In many pagan societies, the earth was seen as a mother, a fertile giver of life. Nature – the soil, forest, sea – was endowed with divinity, and mortals were subordinate to it.
>
> The Judeo-Christian tradition introduced a radically different concept. The earth was the creation of a monotheistic God, who, after shaping it, ordered its inhabitants, in the words of Genesis: 'Be fruitful and multiply, and replenish the earth and subdue it: and have dominion over the fish of the sea and over the fowl of the air and over every living thing that moveth upon the earth.' The idea of

dominion could be interpreted as an invitation to use nature as a convenience. Thus the spread of Christianity, which is generally considered to have paved the way for the development of technology, may at the same time have carried the seeds of the wanton exploitation of nature that often accompanied technical progress.[1]

1. The case against Christianity

The view that Christianity is in some sense responsible for the attitudes and beliefs which have resulted in the environmental crisis did not receive widespread attention until 1967. That year saw the publication of an article entitled 'The Historical Roots of our Ecologic Crisis' by the American historian of science, Lynn White. Since then his article has appeared in numerous anthologies on environmental matters and his thesis has been widely accepted by environmentalists.

He begins by laying the blame for our present environmental problems squarely at the door of western science and technology. This leads him to examine their historical origins and he comes to the conclusion that, 'Since both our technological and our scientific movements got their start, acquired their character, and achieved world dominance in the Middle Ages, it would seem that we cannot understand their nature or their present impact upon ecology without examining fundamental medieval assumptions and developments.'[2]

Many historians of science believe that science as we know it could not have evolved without the particular presuppositions of the Christian doctrine of creation.[3] By directing our attention to the medieval assumptions underlying modern science, White is implicitly aligning himself with this viewpoint. He certainly sees the Middle Ages as a turning point in our relationship with the environment, both technically and intellectually. Technical innovations gave early

[1]*Time*, 2 January, 1989, pp. 17f. [2]L. White, 1967, pp. 1204f.
[3]*E.g.* Funkenstein, 1986; Hooykaas, 1972; C. Russell, 1985.

medieval man greater mastery of his environment. And White suggests that those innovations were inspired by changes in western beliefs about the relationship between humankind and the natural environment; changes connected with the victory of Christianity over paganism.

Having made the link between Christianity and exploitative technologies, White moves on to a critical re-examination of relevant Judaeo-Christian Scriptures as they have been interpreted by western Christianity. He singles out for criticism the biblical understanding of creation and, in particular, the creation stories of Genesis. In Genesis 1 he finds that the human race was created in the image of God and given dominion over the rest of God's creation.

White believes that the latter doctrine reduces nature to a human utility, its sole purpose being to minister to our physical needs: 'God planned all of this explicitly for man's benefit and rule: no item in the physical creation had any purpose save to serve man's purposes.'[1]

At the same time, the former doctrine sets man apart from nature, presenting him as a demi-god with the right and duty to manipulate passive matter:

> Man shares, in great measure, God's transcendence of nature. Christianity, in absolute contrast to ancient paganism and Asia's religions (except, perhaps, Zoroastrianism), not only established a dualism of man and nature but also insisted that it is God's will that man exploit nature for his proper ends.[2]

In White's view the combined effect of these beliefs is to make Christianity 'the most anthropocentric religion the world has seen'.[3] Furthermore, he suggests that the historical nature of the Judaeo-Christian revelation, with its linear view of time, was an important factor in the appearance of doctrines of human progress in western society.

On this analysis, antipathy to the natural world is implicit in the very foundations of the Judaeo-Christian tradition. However, White allows that, 'The implications of Christianity

[1] L. White, 1967, p. 1205. [2] *Ibid.*, p. 1205. [3] *Ibid.*, p. 1205.

for the conquest of nature would emerge more easily in the Western atmosphere.'[1] He also recognizes within the more obviously anti-ecological western tradition, the presence of a positive strand of thought with respect to nature, personified by St Francis of Assisi. St Francis is credited with recognizing that 'all things are fellow creatures praising God in their own ways, as men do in theirs'.[2] For this reason he proposes St Francis as 'a patron saint for ecologists'.[3] Unfortunately, what White gives with one hand, he takes away with the other, asserting that Francis' views were strictly 'heretical'.

More recently White has moderated his argument. Thus, 'All that can be said . . . is that Christianity in its Latin form . . . provided a set of presuppositions remarkably favourable to technological thrust.'[4]

2. The case for the defence

Not surprisingly, White's original accusations and the numerous similar statements published subsequently have elicited a variety of reactions from Christian writers and theologians. Some Christians, particularly those who were already involved in the Green movement, have found his arguments convincing. For them, environmentalism calls into question certain tenets of orthodox Christian belief necessitating a revision of the faith in order to maintain its relevance. Other Christians have taken a more defensive attitude.

The most reactionary response has been to accept White's arguments with a loud 'Hallelujah!' to suppress any sense of disquiet they might cause. Some fundamentalists expect the imminent demise of the earth on biblical grounds and, for them, the environmental crisis is merely additional evidence that God's Kingdom is not of this earth. They argue that since this world will pass away our treatment of it is ultimately a matter of indifference. To such people, Christians who are concerned about the environment have sold out to the New Age movement.[5] Similar reactions have been forthcoming

[1] L. White, 1967, p. 1206. [2] L. White, 1968, p. 100. [3] L. White, 1967, p. 1207. [4] L. White, 1973, p. 58. [5] *E.g.* Cumbey, 1983.

from conservative Roman Catholic circles where environmentalism has been dubbed a new 'American heresy'.[1]

However, the most common reaction has been to attack White's arguments (or his premises) on historical and exegetical grounds.

The *exegetical arguments* mostly focus on White's interpretation of the Genesis creation accounts. In particular, his treatment of Genesis 1:26–28 is called into question.

White, and those who follow him, effectively understand dominion as synonymous with domination. Where Genesis calls the human race to have dominion over the earth, White reads this as a *carte blanche* to dominate and exploit our environment. Thus, 'Christianity made it possible to exploit nature in a mood of indifference to the feelings of natural objects'.[2] In keeping with this view it is sometimes suggested that the biblical command to subdue the earth is couched in the language of victory over an adversary: that humankind is called to trample nature underfoot.

Does the Bible call us to exploit the environment? In declaring that we are God's viceroys on earth, is it granting us the right to act as despots in relation to the rest of creation?

It is true that the Hebrew term 'to subdue' (*radah*) sometimes has oppressive overtones (*e.g.* Ne. 9:28). However, it often merely signifies the normal activity of ruling. In fact, such militaristic terminology was part of the common currency of ancient near-eastern court languages.[3] The biblical scholar James Barr argues that it is this derivative sense which is used in Genesis 1, and he concludes that,

> Human exploitation of animal life is not regarded as an inevitable part of human existence, as something given and indeed encouraged by the ideal conditions of the original creation; at most, it is something that comes along later, after a deterioration in the human condition, as a kind of second best.[4]

Genesis 1 permits the human race to subdue the earth, but this appears to be no more than a warrant for agriculture. We

[1]Schall, 1971, p. 308. [2]L. White, 1967, p. 1205.
[3]Westermann, 1984, p. 159.
[4]Barr, 1972, p. 21.

are given the fruit of the earth to be our food: dominion does not (at this stage) even extend to killing animals for food. The limited nature of the command to have dominion is further reinforced when we recall that the Old Testament's understanding of kingship is very different from the absolute monarchies which evolved in western society.[1] For the ancient Hebrews a ruler existed *for* his subjects:

> As lord of his realm, the king is responsible not only for the realm; he is the one who bears and mediates blessings for the realm entrusted to him. Man would fail in his royal office of dominion over the earth were he to exploit the earth's resources to the detriment of the land, plant life, animals, rivers, and seas.[2]

But the exegetical arguments need not be limited to a direct answer to White's case. As we shall see later, there is much material within the Judaeo-Christian Scriptures which may be drawn on to present a very different picture of biblical attitudes to nature.

No matter how convincing they are, however, exegetical arguments alone will not meet White's case against Christianity. He may be guilty of misinterpreting biblical texts, but the misinterpretation is not his alone. He is merely reproducing a misinterpretation that has been hallowed by frequent repetition in Christian literature and sermons.

To be effective the exegetical arguments must be supplemented. One popular but dangerous approach is to admit the validity of his arguments for some branches of the church, while arguing that one's own tradition has maintained the true Christian approach to the environment. Thus, for example, one Jesuit theologian argues that 'at the origin of the contemporary aggressively exploitative attitude toward the world of nature lies not Christianity as such, but the Christianity of the protestant reformation'.[3]

[1]This is not to imply that the kings of Israel and Judaea always met the standards prescribed in the Old Testament. The history of biblical Israel is a record of the tension between the biblical understanding of kingship and that of the surrounding nations.

[2]Westermann, 1974, p. 52. [3]Faricy, 1987, p. 205.

Any attempt to lay the blame on another strand of Christianity (or one of the philosophies it has spawned) is to admit that a tradition moulded by the Judaeo-Christian Scriptures is indeed responsible for the present situation. It may well be the case that one particular expression of Christianity must bear the responsibility for encouraging an exploitative attitude to nature. But such an argument is incomplete: to avoid guilt by association, the proponent of such an argument must show that a positive Christian theology of nature can be developed.

This brings us to the other line of defence against White: an attack on his *historical arguments*.

One approach is to seek to undermine the force of his criticisms by pointing out that many cultures besides those influenced by the Judaeo-Christian traditions have been guilty of inflicting considerable damage on the environment. Advocating such an approach, Arthur Peacocke asserts that,

> to substantiate White's hypothesis ... it would be necessary to show that men in the 'Judaeo-Christian tradition' have uniquely generated the eco-disasters of our planet; that an exploitative view of nature was actually and generally held in that tradition; and that this tradition actually does involve such an exploitative view.[1]

Thus, apologists for Christianity are apt to recite a litany of non-Christian and, particularly pre-Christian (since advocates of White cannot hope to find evidence of Christian influence on a pre-Christian culture), manmade environmental disasters. Favourite examples include the widespread extinctions caused by fire-drive hunting in pre-Columbian North America; the neolithic and Bronze Age deforestations which transformed much of Northern England into moorland; and the extensive deforestation of Imperial China in spite of the Taoist and Buddhist ideal of adaptation to nature.[2] Clearly, belief in the integrity or even the divinity of nature has by no means precluded widespread environmental damage.

[1]Peacocke, 1979, p. 276.
[2]*E.g.* Peacocke, 1979, p. 277; Yi-Fu, 1970, pp. 244–249.

But to argue in this vein is to miss the real strength of White's argument. As he says himself, 'No sensible person could maintain that all ecologic damage is, or has been, rooted in religious attitudes.'[1] It is illuminating to compare his thesis with Max Weber's correlation of *The Protestant Ethic and the Spirit of Capitalism*. Like White, Weber is often regarded as having argued that a particular body of religious beliefs was the cause of a particular set of human behaviours (in Weber's case that Protestantism caused the rise of capitalism). And, just as examples of pre-Christian exploitation of nature are cited against White, the example of the bankers and merchants of pre-Reformation Lombardy is brought to bear against Weber.

It is arguable, however, that this approach misunderstands both Weber and White. Weber may simply have been trying to establish the existence of structural similarities between Protestantism and capitalism, for example, showing that features of the spirit of Protestant ethics (such as moderation and hard work) were peculiarly suited to promoting aspects of capitalist economics (particularly investment).

Seen in this light, the moderate version of White's case suggests a corresponding functional relationship between Christian teaching with regard to nature and the exploitative practices of significant sections of western society. It is not that western Christianity is the exclusive historical cause of our environmental crisis. Rather, its beliefs were peculiarly well adapted to encouraging the exploitation which has led to the present situation. Thus it is not enough to offer historical counter-examples. Western Christianity still stands accused of being an accessory to our exploitation of the environment. An adequate response to this charge must involve a careful historical examination of the attitudes to nature adopted by the western Christian traditions.

In fact, this weakness of the case for the defence is paralleled by a corresponding weakness in White's case for the prosecution. He makes sweeping assertions about what Christians have believed, without grounding them in real examples. The only Christian he mentions by name is St Francis of Assisi, the chief witness for the defence!

[1]L. White, 1973, p. 57.

An exhaustive historical study of Christian attitudes to nature would be beyond the scope of this book. Instead I shall focus on one Christian thinker who made a seminal contribution to the development of western Christianity (the strand most closely associated with the development of science, technology and the environmental crisis).

3. The example of Augustine

a. *Why Augustine?*

Arguably Augustine is the single most influential figure in the history of western Christian thought.

He was the *éminence grise* behind the intellectual achievements of the Middle Ages. Every medieval theologian was to a greater or lesser degree an Augustinian theologian. St Thomas Aquinas is sometimes picked out as an exception to this general dependence on Augustine. But even Aquinas regarded Augustine as his mentor, and recent studies have revealed that the shape of his theology was much more dependent on Augustine than was previously thought.[1]

As is well known, Augustine was also the guide and inspiration for the Reformers, particularly Luther and Calvin. They regarded him as second only in importance to St Paul.

Nor has his influence waned despite the dramatic changes in theology since the Reformation. It is still visible in the work of theologians as different as Paul Tillich and Karl Barth. And one bibliography cites more than 5,000 studies of his life and work written in the 1950s alone![2]

His interpretation of the doctrine of the Trinity has informed most western discussions of the nature of God and has had a pervasive effect on theology. But his influence extends well beyond theology into western philosophy as a whole. No history of aesthetics, psychology, sociology or politics would be complete without some discussion of his views. And the philosophers of history would point to him as one of the pioneers of the western concept of history.

It is not surprising to discover that he is also regarded as a

[1]*E.g.* Hankey, 1987. [2]Bavel, 1963

seminal figure in the development of western attitudes to the natural world. One recent study of Augustine's attitude to the natural world concludes that 'Augustine . . . was in fact an ecological theologian. His theology was holistic, rather than narrowly anthropocentric.'[1] By contrast, the guru of creation spirituality, Matthew Fox, regards Augustine as the seminal figure of a fall/redemption spirituality: a tradition which, as we shall see later, he regards as responsible for many of the evils of modern society.

From these diametrically opposed assessments it certainly seems that Augustine is a key figure in the development of western Christian attitudes to nature! They also suggest that his own attitude to the natural world was complex. In fact, the study of Augustine's contribution to this issue is greatly complicated by his tortuous spiritual pilgrimage from paganism to Christianity. In response to his experiences he wrote a number of relevant writings which display considerable diversity and development. Thus it is not possible to present a simple uniform picture of his theology of nature.

b. Biographical notes

In order to begin to understand the development of his attitude to the natural world we need to look briefly at the major features of his life history, in particular the religious and intellectual conversions he experienced.

St Augustine was born in the year AD 354 in the North African town of Thagaste. He was the son of a pagan father and a devout Christian mother. Thanks to the patronage of a wealthy uncle he was able to develop his considerable intellectual talents at the university in Carthage. There he soon distinguished himself as an outstanding student of rhetoric. He also underwent his first conversion – to philosophy.

In his autobiographical work, *The Confessions*, he presents this period of his life as one of gross self-indulgence, even libertinism. The reality appears to have been rather less colourful. Probably because of the oppressive influence of his mother, his teenage rebellion was strictly limited in scope. In fact, he rapidly settled into a monogamous relationship with a low class woman who bore him a son, Adeodatus, in 372

[1] Santmire, 1980, p. 182.

and to whom he remained faithful until his conversion to Christianity 14 years later.

He returned to Thagaste briefly after the death of his father. There he found a teaching post in order to support his family. However, the attractions of Carthage (and the proximity of his mother) soon proved too great. By 374 he was once more in Carthage where he set himself up as a professor of rhetoric. Apparently this did not satisfy him for he now began the spiritual quest which was to culminate in his becoming the greatest theologian the Latin church had yet seen. Christianity he dismissed as lacking intellectual credibility. Instead he was attracted to Manicheism: a fashionable, exotic and tantalizingly illusive religious sect. But its greatest attraction for Augustine, the spiritually hungry lover of philosophy, must surely have been its claim to possess secret knowledge about God and the world: knowledge which mediated salvation to its possessors.

From our point of view the significance of this episode is that, after his conversion, much of his early writing about the natural world was in the context of polemics against the sect with which he had once toyed. The Manichees were dualists: for them reality was ultimately a conflict between cosmic forces of good and evil. And the physical universe was merely a projection of that spiritual conflict.

Augustine toyed with this religious philosophy for some nine years. Towards the end of that time his dissatisfaction with Carthage grew until, in 383, he moved to Rome in search of greater influence and more respect for his status as a professor. He stayed there less than a year, moving in 384 to Milan, where he was to take up the post of professor of rhetoric to the city. This was to be the turning point in his life: the finest rhetor of the Manichees was about to cross swords with Bishop Ambrose, the finest rhetor of the Latin church.

For Augustine, the attraction of Ambrose's approach lay in the way he presented Christianity in the context of contemporary philosophy: it could be intellectually credible! In fact, Ambrose and his associates were attempting to express Christian theology in terms of neo-Platonic philosophy. Augustine soon discovered that this synthesis of neo-Platonism and Christianity was far more sophisticated and intellectually satisfying than the crude dualism of the Manichees.

What followed was a period of deep spiritual crisis for Augustine. He was forced to re-examine his motives for evading the claims of the gospel. In 386 he capitulated and became a Christian. Or did he become a neo-Platonist? His early theological works are so heavily influenced by neo-Platonic philosophy that some scholars have spoken of his conversion to neo-Platonism. And throughout his life he showed considerable sympathy for the advocates of this philosophy.

In contrast to the dualism of Manicheism, neo-Platonism was radically monistic: ultimately reality is one. The diversity of creation emanates from the One. However, this emanation was understood as hierarchical, taking place through a Great Chain of Being: the One begets the Intelligence (which contains the Ideas, the forms of all created beings) which, in turn, begets the Soul (the Maker and Governor of the material universe and the repository of all souls). Together these three (the parallel with the Christian doctrine of the Trinity was not lost on Augustine) make up all that is essential in reality. Thus, reality is fundamentally spiritual; matter is attenuated spirit, less real because lower down the Chain of Being; and, because it is less real, matter is also less good (hence Augustine's view that evil was merely the absence of good/being).

But it would be a mistake to write off Augustine as a neo-Platonist in Christian guise. In spite of his sympathy for neo-Platonism, Augustine the theologian and bishop was very conscious of his responsibility to defend and explain the Catholic faith. He viewed neo-Platonism as a valuable tool, but no more. Ultimately the controlling factors in his thought were the Bible and the teachings of the Catholic Church as enshrined in the Nicene Creed not the writings of the neo-Platonists.

c. Augustine's view of the material creation

Thus Augustine's attitude to the natural world was shaped by three factors: his rejection of the Manichean doctrines of his youth, his sympathy for neo-Platonic monism and his adherence to biblical teaching. However, it would be a mistake to think that nature as such was a central issue in his thought. Rather it appears only as a result of polemical and exegetical pressures.

Central to his polemic against Manicheism was his affirmation of the doctrine of *creation from nothing*. This effectively ruled out the Manichean belief that creation was the result of conflict between diametrically opposed cosmic forces.

In spite of his rejection of Manicheism, however, Augustine tends to ignore the goodness of the created order (which is a corollary of the absolute sovereignty of a good Creator). He admits the biblical insistence on the goodness of creation but does not permit it to undermine neo-Platonic doubts about the goodness of matter. At best, the biblical teaching assured him that even the material creation played a part in God's good purposes.

Augustine appears not to have seen any tension between the biblical doctrine of creation and the neo-Platonic view that matter ultimately emanated from the One. Like the neo-Platonists he arranged all reality hierarchically in a Great Chain of Being. In this system spiritual beings are higher, more real, better than material ones.

This is not to say that Augustine believed the material world to be actively evil. On the contrary, even the humblest piece of matter exists only because of its participation in (and, hence, distant resemblance to) the One/God. Thus he was able to accept the biblical affirmation of the goodness of all created reality. Furthermore, it allowed him to recognize the existence of order and beauty even in the material creation.

What is the purpose of the non-human creation? Some of Augustine's writings suggest that the material creation exists primarily to be beautiful and to glorify God. However, the hierarchical streak in his thought means that the lower exists to serve the higher: the material can never be more than a means to a spiritual end. Thus, 'Since the creature . . . is either equal or inferior to us, we must use the inferior for God and enjoy the equal, but in God'.[1] He was quite unable to conceive of nature having order or beauty for its own sake. And, since the human creature is the highest created

[1]Augustine, *Trin.*, 9.8.13.

being in the material realm, it follows that the sub-human creation exists only to serve him.

d. The human and the non-human

Augustine had no difficulty in identifying the sense in which humankind is *the image of God*. Given his hierarchical view of reality, the human soul is the dimension of our being closest to the divine reality. Hence the soul is the image of God.

It follows that the soul is superior to the material creation, and it was to the soul that God addressed the mandate to have dominion over creation. By virtue of its rationality, the human soul is the glory of the world and rightful lord of the irrational creation.

What, then, of his attitude to *the body*? The young Augustine retained some vestiges of the Manichees' hostility to the body. For example, in one early theological treatise he suggests that bodily existence, as such, is a state of fallenness.

This hostility gave way to a more moderate position under the impact of biblical teaching on the matter. Two aspects of the biblical witness were of particular importance in this regard. One was its insistence on the reality of the incarnation: Augustine could not evade the insistence of both Bible and orthodoxy that the Son of God condescended to dwell in an ordinary human body. But, even if that could have been evaded, the Bible's insistence on a general physical resurrection forced him to concede that embodiment is part of God's ultimate plan for us.

Thus, for the mature Augustine, body and soul were distinct but inseparable. However, the superiority of the soul meant that the proper relationship between soul and body could only be that of master to slave.

His hierarchical view of reality shows up again in his understanding of the spiritual life which he envisages as the soul's *ascent to God*. God calls us to eternal rest in the enduring realm of reason. This is the true import of those famous words, 'You made us for yourself and our hearts find no peace until they rest in you.'[1] It follows that love of this world is inappropriate for anyone who has embarked on the spiritual life: 'Life which delights in material joys and

[1]Augustine, *Conf.*, 1.1.

neglects God tends to nothingness and is thereby iniquity.'[1] And,

> we should not vainly behold the beauty of the sky, the order of the stars, the brightness of light, the alternations of day and night, the monthly courses of the moon, the fourfold seasons of the year, the meeting of the four elements, the life-force of seeds begetting forms and numbers, and all things that keep their nature and their appropriate measure each in its own kind. In considering these things there should be no exercise of vain and perishing curiosity, but a step should be taken towards immortal things that abide for ever.[2]

Thus, unlike some of his contemporaries, Augustine did recognize a right use of matter. We are not to enjoy it for its own sake, but rather use it as an instrument for the contemplation of higher things. However, even this is only second best. As an instrument of contemplation nature is to be supplanted by the trinitarian structure of the human soul as soon as one is sufficiently advanced in the spiritual life. Such a view of the religious life naturally lends itself to mere toleration of the physical world while the soul awaits the time of escape from this realm.

e. *Vestiges of a world-affirming theology*

It would be wrong to dismiss Augustine as entirely hostile to the non-human creation. There are clear world-affirming elements in his theology. Unfortunately they are fragmentary and remain largely undeveloped. For example, his insistence on the value of the material creation for the contemplation of God could in another context have become the basis for a more positive Christian assessment of nature.

Further development of his belief in a physical resurrection would ultimately have led to the discarding of the neo-Platonic myth of the fall and return of the soul, and, with it, the rejection of an ascent-oriented spirituality. Thus it would have necessitated the transformation of

[1] Augustine, *Ver.*, 11.22. [2] *Ibid.*, 29.52.

Augustine's anthropology, psychology, aesthetics, spirituality and eschatology!

Amongst the vestiges of a more positive attitude to nature, we might include his very pictorial, even physical analogies for providence. These are sometimes cited as evidence of a change of heart with regard to nature. However, to my mind, a more convincing explanation is that a mismatch has arisen between the theological system he is trying to maintain and his faithfulness to Scripture (the latter resulting in the appearance of rich and moving passages which give a positive place to nature).[1]

4. The ambivalence of western Christianity

Augustine's theology betrays a tension between his faithfulness to Scripture and his commitment to neo-Platonism. To the extent that his successors followed his neo-Platonic insights, western Christian theology has viewed the physical and biological world as inferior to humankind, a resource graciously given to us by God for our use. At the same time it has sought to affirm the biblical doctrine that the non-human creation is good in its own right without reference to the human race. The result has been a pervasive ambivalence towards the natural world.

A recent historical study of western Christian attitudes to the natural world bears witness to the presence of that ambivalence throughout western theology since Augustine's time.[2] It is to be found in the writings of St Thomas Aquinas and St Bonaventure (the first great theologian of the Franciscan Order); in Calvin and Luther; and, more recently, amongst theologians as diverse as Karl Barth, Paul Tillich and Teilhard de Chardin.

The author of the study, Paul Santmire, discerns in western Christian thought about nature two major motifs which he names the Spiritual and the Ecological. The former focuses primarily on God and the soul, or the elect, or the rational creation (humankind and the angels). In theologies

[1] A parallel mismatch is visible between his aesthetic theory and his use of rich imagery in his writings. See O'Connell, 1978.

[2] Santmire, 1985.

shaped by this motif, 'nature tends always to be interpreted or validated (if it is validated) finally in terms of spirit'.[1] The alternative, ecological approach transforms this two-way relationship into a triangular one. Nature is no longer ignored, patronized, or feared. Instead it is seen as the necessary context for encounter with the divine. In such theologies, nature ceases to be incidental to the primary relationship between God and humankind: it, too, is treated as a fundamental parameter.

In a very sympathetic account of Augustine's view, Santmire discerns a gradual shift from the spiritual motif to the ecological in his later writings. However, the dominant view of western Christianity (which White rightly criticizes) may be regarded as the product of an attempt to resolve this ambivalence by suppressing the ecological motif.

Santmire suggests that the ecological motif is capable of accommodating the valid insights of the spiritual motif. Unfortunately, many religious environmentalists conclude that the development of an adequate theology of nature must involve the suppression of the spiritual motif. In doing so they often throw away key elements of the Christian faith. The remaining chapters of this book will be devoted to the development of a Christian approach to the natural world which is both orthodox and capable of meeting the challenge of the environmental crisis.

[1]Santmire, 1985, p. 9.

CHAPTER THREE

The spiritual dimension of environmentalism

1. From ecology to Green spirituality

Until relatively recently it would have seemed incongruous to speak of environmentalism as having a spiritual dimension. Even now many environmentalists are embarrassed by the suggestion, perhaps feeling that their status as political and economic activists is compromised by being associated with a form of mysticism. Nevertheless, over the past three decades there has been a gradual change in how environmentalism is perceived. A Green spirituality has emerged from what originally appeared to be a secular pressure group, inspired primarily by scientific considerations (albeit, with socialist overtones). At first this was generally dismissed as a lunatic fringe. Today, however, the Green movement is seen widely as a bearer and advocate of important spiritual and ethical values.

There are two equal and opposite errors into which Christian observers of the environmentalist scene may fall. One is to assume that all environmentalists take a spiritual approach to the issue – that it is simply a revival of earth mysticism. The other is to accept the propaganda of political environmentalists who would still have us believe that environmental spirituality concerns only a lunatic fringe of the movement.

a. Analysing the environmentalist spectrum

To put the spiritual dimension of environmentalism in perspective we need to look briefly at the tremendous diversity to be found within the movement. Ecological anxieties have united men and women of every conceivable political, economic and religious persuasion. The result is a remarkably diffuse movement which defies easy description.

However, the diversity (not to mention internal conflict) becomes clear as soon as we begin to probe beneath the surface with appropriate questions.

For example, we may ask what they believe about social change. Are they revolutionaries or reformers? Do they believe that human societies are stable conservative systems in which radical change is naturally suppressed? If so, they are likely to advocate a revolutionary approach to environmentalism: individuals must be 'converted' to a Green perspective, and present human societies must be overthrown to make way for a Green Utopia. Other environmentalists regard society as more flexible: they see it as an organic open system which is, perhaps to a limited extent, responsive to major changes in its circumstances. Thus they can conceive of present societies evolving appropriate responses to the global environmental crisis. Clearly this will result in environmentalist tactics quite different from those of the revolutionaries. Equally clearly this is not a simple either/or. Individuals and groups will differ in the extent to which they hold one or other view.

Another way of classifying environmentalists would be to ask about their understanding of human freedom. To what extent does the environment influence human behaviour? For those who regard its influence as substantial, humankind is essentially a part of nature or subordinate to nature. In fact, most committed environmentalists are environmental determinists to some extent. This is probably because most contemporary secular philosophies which stress freewill tend to do so in terms of a contrast between human behaviour and nature. Thus freedom is understood as the capacity to act against one's natural conditioning.

b. Ecocentric or technocentric?

One very fundamental division within environmentalism is over the role of technology in responding to the environmental crisis. Those who believe that a technological solution is possible have been described as technocentric environmentalists.[1] Such people mostly remain outside the popular environmental pressure groups and may not even be recognized as environmentalists by members of those groups.

The values of technocentric environmentalists are those of western industrial society: they emphasize efficiency, rationality, human progress and control of the environment. These are men and women who have espoused the environmental cause for utilitarian reasons. O'Riordan summarizes their approach as, 'the orderly exploitation of resources for the greatest good of the greatest number over the longest time, the prevention of waste and the control of the earth for the good of man'.[2]

It would be churlish to deny that such people are genuinely concerned about our impact on the environment. However, their ideology is a far cry from that of the Green Party. Technocentrism is, essentially, the response of western technological materialism to the environmental crisis.

In contrast to the managerial efficiency of technocentrism, ecocentric environmentalism is characterized by a sense of wonder, reverence and moral obligation. But responsibility to whom or what? Technocentrism is unashamedly anthropocentric: we are responsible to our fellow human beings (and, possibly, our posterity) for our treatment of the environment. However, for ecocentric environmentalists (popularly known as Greens) our moral obligation is to the earth itself: respect for non-human life is a cornerstone of their ethics. Ecocentrism lies behind many of the typical expressions of popular environmentalism, including an enthusiasm for low-impact

[1]O'Riordan, 1981, p. 11. [2]*Ibid.*, p. 12.

ology, emphases on self-reliance and the advocacy ghts for animals. The ecocentric or Green outlook is d summarized in Jonathon Porritt's personal manifesto:

- a reverence for the Earth and for all its creatures;
- a willingness to share the world's wealth among all its peoples;
- prosperity to be achieved through sustainable alternatives to the rat race of economic growth;
- lasting security to be achieved through non-nuclear defence strategies and considerably reduced arms spending;
- a rejection of materialism and the destructive values of industrialism;
- a recognition of the rights of future generations in our use of all resources;
- an emphasis on socially useful, personally rewarding work, enhanced by human-scale technology;
- protection of the environment as a precondition of a healthy society;
- an emphasis on personal growth and spiritual development;
- respect for the gentler side of human nature;
- open, participatory democracy at every level of society;
- recognition of the crucial importance of significant reductions in population levels;
- harmony between people of every, race, colour and creed;
- a non-nuclear, low-energy strategy, based on conservation, greater efficiency and renewable sources;
- an emphasis on self-reliance and decentralized communities.[1]

c. *Shades of Green*

In spite of the fact that Jonathon Porritt can publish a

[1]Porritt, 1984, p. 39.

Green manifesto that is capable of attracting widespread support from Greens (and, indeed, from many who would not align themselves with the Green movement), ecocentrism is not a single coherent phenomenon. On the contrary, there are many shades of Green!

For example, the entire political spectrum is represented within ecocentric environmentalism. At one extreme are the so-called ecofascists (or neo-Malthusians) who put great emphasis on the conservative implications of Thomas Malthus' classic, *Essay on the Principle of Population*. The heart of his essay was the contention that, since natural resources are finite, there must be a finite upper limit to the population which may be supported by those resources. Today, this view is often associated with the life-boat ethic.

At the other extreme are a variety of left-wing and radical viewpoints, often expressed in community lifestyles. One of the early inspirations of this brand of ecocentrism was the work of the anarchist Peter Kropotkin. Between those extremes ecocentric opinions can be found in every political party. However, it would be accurate to describe the Green Party and its continental counterparts as advocating a radical form of socialism.

There are equally deep differences over whether there is a spiritual dimension to environmentalism. Many ecosocialists are very suspicious of Green spirituality (especially in Germany, where they recall with horror the Nazi use of earth mysticism). By contrast, the Deep Ecology movement sees spirituality as a vital aspect of environmental concern, without which environmentalism degenerates into mere conservation. The bitterness of this division is made clear by a leading ecosocialist, Murray Bookchin:

> The greatest difference that is now emerging in the so-called 'Ecology Movement' today is between a vague, formless, self-contradictory, invertebrate thing called 'Deep Ecology', and a long-developing, coherent, socially-oriented body of ideas that is best called Social Ecology. Deep Ecology has parachuted into our midst quite recently from the sun-belt's bizarre mix of Hollywood and Disneyland, re-born Christianity, spiced homilies from Taoism, Bud-

> dhism, spirituality and so on and so forth.[1]

Equally tendentious, but more descriptive, are the following comments from Australian philosopher John Passmore:

> 'Depth' ... implies an acceptance of primitivism and mysticism, a willingness to revert to a state of affairs where the world, except for a few colonies of hunters, was a vast wilderness, the rejection, as 'speciesism', of any preference for human interests over the interests of any other species.[2]

d. Green spirituality

In spite of Bookchin's attempts to dismiss Deep Ecology as 'ecolala' or 'nebulous nature-worship with its suspicious bouquet of wood-sprites and fertility rites, its animist, shamanistic figures and post-industrial paganism',[3] the spiritual dimension of Green politics is arguably one of the features which makes it attractive to voters. An editorial in *Green Christians* commented that 'One well-heeled elderly lady of cautious disposition was overheard to say at a garden party that she favoured the Green Party because it alone, among the contenders [for the European elections], appeared to care about spiritual values.'

But what is the meaning of spirituality in this context? It should be stressed that recognition of a spiritual dimension to environmental issues does not imply any degree of sympathy for the Christian faith. On the contrary, as we have already seen, many environmentalists are highly critical of Christianity's attitude to the environment.

Today the term spirituality is used 'to describe those attitudes, beliefs and practices which animate people's lives and help them to reach out towards super-sensible realities'.[4] It implies that those who are interested in such matters are not satisfied with the crude materialism of our present age. However, neither the beliefs nor the realities to which they point are necessarily Christian. As Gordon Wakefield points out, 'Adolf Hitler was a spiritual being, a man, more than

[1]Porritt & Winner, 1988, p. 236. [2]Passmore, 1980, p. ix.
[3]Porritt & Winner, 1988, p. 238.
[4]*NDCT*, p. 549.

most, "possessed"; yet his spirit was surely evil.'[1] In the light of such an example, Christians dare not suspend their responsibility to 'test the spirits to see whether they are from God' (1 Jn. 4:1), even if Green spirituality does appear to be more benign than National Socialism.

Like so many other aspects of popular environmentalism, Green spirituality is a loose coalition rather than a coherent movement (much less a set of doctrines). One religiously motivated Green discovers that another Green shares his or her motivation and discussion centres on how their respective religious beliefs have led to this convergence of concern. One may be a Christian and the other a Buddhist but they may find that they have more in common with each other than with their co-religionists.[2] Some religious traditions (*e.g.* the many forms of witchcraft and shamanism) have always put great emphasis on the earth. Other philosophies and religions have latched on to aspects of environmentalism as an effective way of conveying their beliefs and practices to a wider audience and as a means of achieving legitimacy.[3]

What are we to make of such a pot-pourri? In what remains of this chapter I shall attempt to analyse the clearly non-Christian forms of Green spirituality, looking first at some of the sources from which they seek inspiration and then at major common themes.

2. Some sources of Green spirituality

a. The perennial philosophy

A major source of inspiration for Green spirituality has been what Aldous Huxley called the perennial philosophy. He sought common themes within a wide range of eastern and

[1] *NDCT*, p. 549.

[2] The origins of the Christian Ecology Group reflect just such a process. It began in 1981 when someone stood up during a Green Party Conference and asked if anyone would be interested in holding a prayer meeting. The outcome is one of the most ecumenical groupings within British Christianity, representing many denominations and many different perspectives within those denominations. What keeps them together is their common commitment to a Christian perspective on the environment.

[3] *E.g.* The Hunger Project, inspired by Werner Erhard's EST.

western religious and philosophical traditions. What he found was a common mystical understanding of the cosmos and our place within it. According to this point of view, 'our narrow isolated socialized self is an illusion . . . in reality, we are intimately connected with the natural processes around us'.[1] The concept of being intimately related to nature is, of course, close to the heart of Greens.

Huxley has pointed them both westwards and eastwards in their quest for philosophical and religious underpinning for their position. The move eastwards is a familiar one which has been occurring with increasing frequency for the past century. In particular, Taoism and Buddhism are often singled out as religious traditions which support an ecocentric view of life. However, they tend to be viewed in a very uncritical way. For example, it is rarely recognized that Chinese and Japanese Buddhists engaged in wholesale deforestation during the Middle Ages.[2]

Less well known is the turn to other western traditions. In particular, the search for a philosophy to underpin Deep Ecology has focused on Baruch Spinoza (a Dutch Jewish philosopher of the seventeenth century). His unorthodox views led to his expulsion from the Synagogue. After his death his writings were to be influential in shaping the thought of key liberal Christian theologians, notably Friedrich Schleiermacher. The aspect of his philosophy most relevant to environmental issues is surely his pantheism. In fact, what little he says about environmental ethics is embarrassingly anthropocentric – he was still very much a child of his times. Nevertheless, several influential Deep Ecologists, including George Sessions and Arne Naess, insist that his system is ecocentric.

b. Romanticism and transcendentalism

Romanticism emerged in the late eighteenth century as a reaction against the crudely mechanistic view of nature advocated by the philosophers of the European Enlightenment and expressed in the rise of industrial capitalism. The Romantics rejected Newtonian science and the materialism of the day, stressing instead the freedom of the individual

[1]Devall & Sessions, 1985, p. 80. [2]Yi-Fu, 1970, pp. 244–249.

(often in terms of human creativity as against the alienation created by industrial working practices). They also gave birth to the reverence for simplicity and idealization of the past which are to be found in 'back to nature' movements to this day.

Some of them undoubtedly tended towards a vague pantheism in their reverence for nature. However, several leading Romantics remained clearly within the Christian tradition. There can be little doubt about William Blake's commitment to Christianity, albeit a rather unorthodox mystical form. As for Coleridge, he was arguably the finest English theologian of his generation and far more orthodox than he is usually thought to be.

In many ways transcendentalism was a mid-nineteenth century American replay of European Romanticism. Its best-known exponents were Ralph Waldo Emerson and Henry David Thoreau. The latter, in particular, exerted a tremendous influence on American attitudes to nature through his own writings and through the life and work of his disciple, John Muir.

The name of their movement reflects the fact that fundamental to their thought was a belief in the transcendence of mind over nature. This may seem a strange starting point for an ecocentric philosophy. However, they also saw nature as symbolic of spirit. The practical outcome was a deep appreciation of the natural world and a rejection of what they saw as the manipulative attitude of their contemporaries. Some words of Thoreau sum up this attitude: 'In wilderness is the preservation of the world.'[1]

In the case of John Muir this appreciation of nature became a radical questioning of anthropocentrism reminiscent of today's Deep Ecologists: 'If a war of races should occur between the wild beasts and Lord Man, I would be tempted to sympathize with the bears ...', or 'Why ought man to value himself as more than an infinitely small composing unit of the one great unit of creation?'[2] Again we see the stress on the interconnectedness of all things.

[1]Quoted in Wilkinson, 1980, p. 141.
[2]Quoted in Devall & Sessions, 1985, p. 104.

c. Primal religious traditions

As I have already mentioned, many of the animistic or shamanistic religions stress the affinity between humankind and the earth. In recent years this has attracted the attention of those searching for a Green spirituality.

In North America there is considerable interest in Native American spirituality, at least in part because of its Green implications. Today a book on environmentalism would seem incomplete without some reference to Chief Seattle's 1851 surrender speech: 'One thing we know for sure: the earth was not made for man, man was made for the earth.'

The North American Indian attitude to nature may be summed up thus: 'In the Circle of Life every being is no more or less, than any other. We are all Sisters and Brothers. Life is shared with the bird, bear, insects, plants, mountains, clouds, stars, sun. To be in harmony with the natural world, one must live within the cycles of life.'[1]

d. Ecology?

Deep Ecology and Green spirituality have certainly capitalized on the public perception that environmentalism is scientific because of its connections with ecology. However, the detailed results of ecological research are of relatively little interest to them. Instead they value the direct contact with the natural world which engagement in ecological studies permits. They see this as helping people to understand 'the need to go beyond the narrow definition of scientific data and look to their own consciousness to develop their own sense of place.'[2]

Having said that, it should be added that there is one point at which they believe ecology has made a real contribution to Green spirituality. This is the rediscovery of the principle of interconnectedness: that everything is related to everything else.[3]

e. Conclusions

It will be clear from this very brief outline of some of the influences on Deep Ecology and Green spirituality that it is an incredibly eclectic movement. There is a readiness to draw

[1]Steiner, 1976, p. 113. [2]Devall & Sessions, 1985, p. 85. [3]*Ibid.*

on anything which may give further spiritual depth to environmentalism. However, underlying that eclecticism there does seem to be a principle of selection, a common factor in the various spiritual and philosophical strands mentioned above. It is the agreement on a holistic perspective, on interconnectedness.

3. Interconnectedness

a. Evolution and the Great Chain of Being

We often talk about Darwin's theory of evolution as if evolution itself was Darwin's idea. But that is not so. Evolutionary ideas were already widespread when Darwin began to think about the origin of the diversity of species. And prior to the publication of *The Origin of Species* several important volumes had already been published on the topic.[1]

In fact, some people traced the idea of evolution right back to the philosophies of ancient Greece and Rome (for example, Matthew Arnold wrote of the debate about evolution, 'I cannot understand why you scientific people make such a fuss about Darwin. Why, it's all in Lucretius!'). It seems unlikely that ideas like those of Darwin, Lamarck or Chambers are to be found in classical philosophy. However, there is a common underlying theme, namely, the Great Chain of Being.

This was an elaborate metaphysical schema purporting to show the relationship of all entities to each other and to God. The raw materials for the scheme are to be found in the philosophies of Plato and Aristotle, but it was neo-Platonism (which, as we have seen, so influenced Augustine) which finally organized them into a single coherent system. Augustine's contemporary, Macrobius, summarizes the doctrine thus:

> Since, from the Supreme God, Mind arises, and from Mind, Soul, and since this in turn creates all

[1]These include Erasmus Darwin's *Zoonomia* (London, 1794); the Chevalier de Lamarck's theory of acquired characteristics (1809); and Robert Chambers' anonymous but highly influential *Vestiges of the Natural History of Creation* (1844).

> subsequent things and fills them all with life, and since this single radiance illumines all and is reflected in each, as a single face might be reflected in many mirrors placed in a series; and since all things follow in continuous succession, degenerating in sequence to the very bottom of the series, the attentive observer will discover a connection of parts, from the Supreme God down to the last dregs of things, mutually linked together and without a break. And this is Homer's golden chain, which God, he says, bade hang down from heaven to earth.[1]

Thus all of creation, from the most glorious archangel to the lowliest particle of dust, is envisaged as interrelated in a single hierarchical structure emanating from the One. The extent to which it has penetrated western thought is clear when we look at how natural the hierarchy still seems to be. We still speak of 'higher' mammals and 'lower' invertebrates. In many religious circles it seems natural to regard purely spiritual beings (angels) as 'higher' than embodied spirits (humans) and those in turn as 'higher' than non-rational animals. Lowest of all is disordered matter, chaos, flux.

Within this metaphysical framework Arthur Lovejoy[2] has identified three key characteristics:

i. The principle of plenitude: every niche in reality is filled with entities. This implies

ii. Continuity: all gaps will be filled. In the words of Plutarch, 'Nature abhors a vacuum.'

iii. The principle of gradation: the relationship of entities to one another is a hierarchy of perfection with God at the apex.

In western Christian thought the doctrine of creation succeeded in breaking the Chain of Being by denying the emanation of all things from God. But the elaborate hierarchical structure of creation remained intact. It is part of the cultural baggage that we share with Darwin. For example, John Wesley suggests all three of Lovejoy's principles in the following,

[1]Quoted in Lovejoy, 1936, p. 63. [2]Lovejoy, 1936.

> The whole Progress of Nature is so gradual, that the entire Chasm from Plant to Man is filled up with divers Kinds of Creatures, rising one above another by so gentle an Ascent that the Transitions from one Species to another are almost insensible.[1]

By this time the Great Chain of Being had been institutionalized within the infant science of biology. All that had changed was the imagery: the tree of life. It reached its highest degree of sophistication with Carl von Linne's hierarchical system of biological classification: a system which is almost universally accepted to this day.

But if evolutionary ideas are so closely related to this Chain of Being, why did it take so long for them to appear? Why is there a gap of a millennium and a half between the neo-Platonists and the first explicit evolutionists? To understand this we must recall the dramatic change in our understanding of history and time which took place in the eighteenth century.

Until the Reformation there was no real consciousness of history in European thought. People wrote chronicles and histories of sorts but there was no recognition that time might change things. Artists painted pictures on historical themes but the architecture and dress was contemporary. Playwrights wrote historical plays (*e.g. Julius Caesar*) but the issues they tackled were contemporary ones. It was assumed that the structures of society and culture were fixed by divine decree just as, in biology, the number of species was fixed.

The Reformation brought with it a much greater emphasis on divine providence and (since Augustine had already associated providence with history) hence on history. With the Enlightenment came a reaction against all forms of authoritarianism which led people to question the divine status of social structures. If societies are human rather than divine then they are as impermanent as we are: people became aware that societies might exist with quite different sets of values and different ways of organizing themselves. The authority of divine decree gave way to the authority of

[1]From Wesley's *Survey of the Wisdom of God in Creation*, cited by Blackmore & Page, 1989, p. 13.

human reason and the Christian doctrine of divine providence was supplanted by the secular doctrine of inexorable progress. If human societies really have changed over periods of time, the simplest way to make sense of this is to look for progress.

By the turn of the nineteenth century most people (including most theologians) took it for granted that human progress and divine providence were one and the same. Evolutionary speculation was simply the extension of the doctrine of progress to the non-human. In Lovejoy's language, evolutionary thought was the temporalization of the Great Chain of Being.

What has this to do with Green spirituality and the principle of interconnectedness? Simply this: the Great Chain of Being assumes that all entities are interconnected (albeit, in a hierarchical fashion). Darwinism tamed and curtailed the principle – it proposed a mechanism for how this might happen in the real world and reduced a philosophical principle to a scientific hypothesis. Interconnectedness remained a part of Darwin's conceptual armoury.

In addition to seeing a temporal Chain of Being, Darwin was aware of the interdependence of living beings and even spoke of them as being 'bound together by a web of complex relations'.[1] Such concepts were to lead Darwin's young German disciple, Ernst Haeckel, to coin the word 'ecology', and, unwittingly, lay the foundations for twentieth-century environmentalism.

b. From Gaia to planetary consciousness

I introduced the Gaia hypothesis in chapter 1 as one particularly forceful model of a global ecosystem. It is relevant in this context because it probably represents the boundary line of interconnectedness as a scientific rather than a metaphysical principle.

Arguing from the insights of systems theory, Jim Lovelock (the originator of the hypothesis) has proposed an intriguing new way of looking at the relationship between organisms and their abiotic environment. It is generally agreed that the environment has a profound influence upon organisms and

[1]Darwin, 1928, p. 75.

their evolution – species must adapt to their environments, the ones which adapt most successfully are most likely to persist. Lovelock's hypothesis asserts that the converse is also true: on a global scale, organisms profoundly influence their abiotic environment in such a way as to maintain that environment as close to an optimum for the continuance of life as possible. In other words, the evolution of life has resulted in a biosphere which functions on a global scale as an active control system.

The Gaia hypothesis is an intriguing way of looking at the global ecosystem. It appears to be testable, and it certainly offers a range of fresh insights into old problems. However, it has become a focus of controversy because of the way it has been received by the advocates of Green spirituality.

Lovelock himself remains within the discipline of the scientific method. He seeks to test his hypothesis and has devised increasingly sophisticated computer models to demonstrate that the assumption of an entirely unconscious coupling between the global ecosystem and its abiotic environment does result in an extremely stable system.

By contrast, the New Age movement has taken it up as an important religious myth because of its apparent affinity with the concept of planetary consciousness.[1] This concept is understood in a variety of ways. In its more moderate forms it represents a spiritualization of the international world order dreamt of by socialists of past generations. More extreme versions envisage the emergence of a single planetary brain of which human beings are the brain cells. The Gaia hypothesis has allowed them to create the impression that this concept is rooted in serious biology. They simply draw an analogy between the complexity of a mammalian central nervous system and that of Gaia.

The Green/New Age adoption of Gaian consciousness represents the unharnessing of interconnectedness from the scientific disciplines imposed upon it by Darwin and his contemporaries. Freed from rational criticism and empirical testing, interconnectedness can function once more as a fundamental philosophical concept and (in its Gaian form) as a religious myth.

[1]Important advocates of Gaian consciousness include Pedler, 1979 and P. Russell, 1982.

c. *Some implications of interconnectedness*

More generally, the principle of interconnectedness relates everything to everything else; all spiritual and material realities are made mutually interdependent; but without the hierarchical component of the older doctrine. The Great Chain of Being has been revived, but it no longer hangs down from heaven to earth. It has been tied in upon itself in countless ways – more of a Gordian knot than a chain.

Apart from the insistence that humankind is an integral part of the natural world, the principle finds expression in a variety of holistic philosophies and therapies. A corollary is the contemporary tendency to repudiate the analytic, reductionistic techniques which have been the mainstay of western science. Thus Deep Ecologists have tended to present ecology as a radical departure from traditional science. More generally, Greens and others who assume the principle of interconnectedness are highly critical of all forms of reductionism. This is often accompanied by interest in alternative ways of knowing (*e.g.* mysticism of all sorts) and a tolerance of pluralism with respect to belief systems.

Other aspects of western culture also come under fire from this partial revival of the Hellenistic worldview. For example, acceptance of the principle entails the rejection of western individualism in favour of greater collectivism. It is no coincidence that some of the most outstanding examples of putting Green beliefs into practice, of 'living at peace with the planet', are to be found in contemporary experiments in communal lifestyle. The stress on communality is a corollary of the fundamental presupposition of the Green outlook.

Unguarded application of the principle to human relationships, however, can easily lead to the authoritarian subordination of the individual to the whole. The principle of interconnectedness would have been as attractive to a thinking Nazi as it is to Greens. The totalitarian potential of this aspect of Green thought is well demonstrated by Callenbach's environmentalist novel, *Ecotopia*: there it is envisaged that only a fascist state could successfully impose the radical measures necessary to achieve an environmental Utopia.

Another implication of the principle is the rejection of mind-body dualism. Matter and spirit are inextricably bound up together.

4. Pantheism

a. From holism to pantheism

Clearly the principle of interconnectedness has important theological implications. It introduces a strongly pantheistic tendency into Green spirituality.

All things are inextricably linked together to form a Whole. It takes little imagination to envisage the Whole as a coherent system in its own right. This is simply an extension of the Gaian/planetary consciousness concept described above.[1] However, people who adopt this line of argument are likely to find the notion of a transcendent Other quite incomprehensible. What can it mean to talk of God the Creator as wholly other, as somehow standing over against creation? To them it can mean only that Christians are not taking the system as a whole. The Whole, for them, must be Creator and creation understood as a single system.

Like most philosophy since the Enlightenment, there is no room for a transcendent God in holistic thinking of this sort. Unlike the philosophers of the Enlightenment, however, the advocates of Green spirituality are unhappy with the notion of Man as the measure of all things. If there is no transcendent God, and Man will not do as a substitute, where should we look for an appropriate object of worship? The answer is clear: we must look to the Whole, we must become pantheists.

Thus one writer on Green spirituality begins by speaking of a '"creation spirituality", which honors the natural world as the most profound expression of the Divine'. But, less than fifty pages later, she is saying 'the Godhead must be considered female as well as male. . . . Being forced to say "God the Mother" once in a while is pointless if people have in mind Yahweh-with-a-skirt. We must first understand who She is: She is not in the sky; *She is earth.*'[2]

b. Monism or pluralism?

Mention of pantheism immediately brings to mind the monistic outlook of eastern mysticism. According to such

[1]Lovelock himself explicitly rejects such an extension of his hypothesis, *e.g.* Lovelock, 1988, p. 206.

[2]Spretnak, 1986, pp. 17, 62f. *My emphasis.*

philosophies, the Whole (or the One) is ultimate reality. How is this related to our experience of the world in all its manifold complexity? The monist will respond that the complexity of the world is an illusion. What is real is our oneness. Mythological explanations abound about the origins of the illusory complexity we call the world: it is the dream of God, or the madness of God.

It will be clear that a consistent monistic philosophy will have little to say about the environmental crisis. When we allow ourselves to be worried by environmental problems we are merely letting ourselves be deluded by an illusion. The right course of action is not to respond to the crisis but rather to seek enlightenment: identification of self with the One.

Many western forms of pantheism, however, are pluralistic rather than pantheistic. In affirming the deity of the Whole they refuse to deny the reality of the many. On the contrary, the Whole and the many are understood to be mutually dependent. This is true of neo-Platonism in which the emanation of all things from the One and their subsequent return is seen as an enrichment of the One.

A similar outlook is found in contemporary witchcraft. The influential American witch, Starhawk, expresses it thus:

> All things are one, yet each is separate, individual, unique. . . . The world of separate things is the reflection of the One, the One is the reflection of the myriad separate things of the world. We are all 'swirls' of the same energy, yet each swirl is unique in its own form and pattern.[1]

A pantheism which acknowledges the uniqueness of each component part of the whole is in a much stronger position to address the environmental crisis than one which denies their reality. It is able to recognize the importance for the harmonious functioning of the Whole of each entity. Thus each creature comes to be seen as being of equal value. The result is an ethic which accords equal rights to the land and its life forms. It leads to a lifestyle which has been summed up in the slogan 'living lightly on the land'.

[1]Starhawk, 1979, p. 25.

c. Critique

Ironically, it remains questionable whether pantheism is conducive to responsible care for the environment. Strange as it may seem, western pluralistic pantheism has a long historical association with gnosticism and its antipathy towards material reality. All things may be divine but, too often, some things are seen as more divine than others. Overt statements about the divine status of all reality have often masked covert beliefs about the divinity of man (or, rather, of some men). What saves Green spirituality from the anti-environmental implications of consistent pantheism is its eclecticism (which, at times, verges on a celebration of inconsistency).

Speaking from a Christian perspective, I find pantheistic spirituality unsatisfactory because it seems to leave little room for personhood. Human beings appear as islands of subjectivity in a basically impersonal cosmos and many of the techniques of pantheistic spirituality appear to be designed to suppress my individual self-consciousness in favour of closer identification with the Whole. With no clear distinction between God and the world, it is hard to distinguish pantheism from a religious form of atheism.

Its answer to the problem of evil also leaves much to be desired. Evil is merely the result of ignorance. If people understood their true relation to each other and to the cosmos, they would behave in more loving, more environmentally-friendly ways.

Of course, this means that salvation is a matter of education. Why then are we not all enlightened? It can only be because the process of education is a long and arduous one – one that cannot be completed in a single lifetime. The concepts of reincarnation and karma (the law of cause-and-effect which drives the cycle of reincarnation) may not be logical implications of pantheism but they certainly sit easily with it.

CHAPTER FOUR

Christian responses to the environmental crisis

1. Introduction

Growing awareness of the environmental crisis and the more recent emergence of Green spirituality have resulted in a tremendous variety of responses from the Christian community. Broadly speaking, they can be classified into one of three categories: reaction, reconstruction, or re-examination.

i. Reaction: This is the response of those who perceive Green spirituality as a serious threat to Christianity. Typically they respond negatively to the adverse criticisms of traditional Christian thought and practice in relation to the environment even when there is some justification for those criticisms. In some cases they refuse to admit the seriousness of the environmental crisis, perhaps arguing that environmentalism diverts us from more urgent matters such as evangelism.

ii. Reconstruction: This is the polar opposite of a reactionary rejection of environmentalism. Christians in this category have accepted the environmentalist critique of Christianity, failing to see that there have always been elements within the

Christian tradition which affirm the non-human creation. Despairing of orthodox Christianity, they pin their hopes on some reconstruction of the faith which might modify it in the direction of greater environmental friendliness. They are likely to perceive Green spirituality as a resource upon which to draw in the task of reconstruction rather than as a threat. One might describe their response as a capitulation to the Spirit of the Age.

Three of the responses examined in this chapter fall into this category: process theology, theologies based on the work of Teilhard de Chardin and Matthew Fox's creation-centred spirituality.

iii. Re-examination: There is a middle way. We can admit the force of environmentalist criticisms of some Christian traditions without compromising the fundamental tenets of Christian belief. Such an approach recognizes the historical diversity of the Christian religion and the existence within that diversity of traditions which retained a positive attitude to the environment. It will re-examine those traditions and their biblical roots in order to find resources with which to address the present crisis. The rest of this book is a modest attempt at such an exercise.[1]

2. Technocentric reactions

Strictly speaking, both this and the next section are about Christian *reactions* to the environmental crisis. Wholesale revision is as much a reaction as the conservatism examined here. However, the two kinds of reaction are so different it is convenient to treat them separately for the sake of clarity.

The conservative reaction is to look at Green philosophy and spirituality, recognize its affinities with paganism and then dismiss the whole environmentalist agenda as a front for neo-paganism. In its most extreme pre-millennial forms this reaction actually celebrates the environmental crisis as one more piece of evidence that the End is nigh. Of course, this is simply a corollary of the view that a nuclear holocaust might

[1]It is by no means the first such attempt. Others include Hendry, 1980; Moltmann, 1985; and Santmire, 1985.

be God's way of ushering in the return of Christ.

Incredible as it may seem, some Christians do adopt such a view. Constance Cumbey is a Detroit-based attorney who is well known for her campaign against the New Age movement. While she does not address the environmental issue directly, her views are only too clear in her critique of a major evangelical report on the environment.[1]

The notion that we might have any responsibility for the earth is clearly anathema to her. We should not seek any reconciliation between humankind and nature since 'If I read my Bible correctly, our peace was to be with God – not nature.'[2] Ultimately nature is dispensable for 'God was going to create all things new – not redeem nature along with man.'[3]

However, the thrust of her argument (and its location in a volume on the New Age movement) makes it clear that her concern is not so much with nature as with the dangers of environmentalism. She is clearly horrified at the extent to which Calvin College has compromised its theology in associating itself with this volume. What began as an examination of Christian stewardship of natural resources has become a vehicle for 'The New Age political program . . . in its entirety – including a *duty* for Christians to support globalization of our structures.'[4]

Because of their efforts to articulate a theology of nature, she accuses the authors of monism. The 'climax' is her deliberate misrepresentation of the book as advocating a new world religion (and implying a bias towards Hindu occultism).[5]

Why do some Christians take such an extreme view? And why do they go to such lengths to blacken the reputations of Christians who take a different view? Could it be that the centre of their faith is not Christ himself but rather his imminent return? Thus anything which might be seen as hindering the imminent end of the world (working for peace

[1]Cumbey, 1983, pp.162–169. She attacks Wilkinson, 1980, a report by fellows of the Calvin Center for Christian Scholarship.

[2]Cumbey, 1983, p. 163. [3]*Ibid.* [4]*Ibid.*, pp. 162f.

[5]*Ibid.*, p. 168. The passage on which she bases her accusation (Wilkinson, 1980, p. 222) has been taken out of context and edited. Originally it referred not to Hinduism but Eastern Orthodox Christianity!

and justice, famine relief, environmentalism) is perceived as an attack on the very heart of their faith.

3. Are creation and nature compatible?

A more measured response to the current popularity of theologies of nature has come from the American theologian, Gordon Kaufman.[1] He expresses doubts about whether the concept of nature is compatible with an authentic Christian theology. Could it be that, by adopting the idea of nature, we are importing into our theology an alien concept that will ultimately compromise the distinctives of the Christian faith? He offers a salutary reminder that theologians must always be self-critical of their use of non-biblical concepts.

The first thing to notice about the concept of nature is its multivalence.[2] Because of the extreme complexity of its usage, Kaufman examines only its use in such phrases as 'the order of nature' and 'the natural world'. Here he observes an ambiguity which goes beyond mere linguistic confusion. Nature can mean everything – the totality of powers and processes (including man and all his works). But it can also mean whatever is not part of human culture – wilderness. Taking the latter as his starting point, Kaufman defines nature as

> the widest context of human life, and thus our most fundamental home, viewed as wilderness ('untouched by human hand') rather than on some analogy or image drawn from the teleological and meaning-filled orders of society and culture.[3]

Understood in this way, nature is a relatively concrete, immediate concept. We can experience it in a way that is not possible for a concept such as 'world'. But this means that it

[1]Kaufman, 1981, pp. 209–237.

[2]Lovejoy & Boas, 1935, pp. 447–456, lists some thirty-nine literary and philosophical uses of nature and a further twenty-seven ethical, political and religious uses derived from them.

[3]Kaufman, 1981, p. 218.

readily becomes an object of religious devotion – an idol. Kaufman's argument is apparently confirmed by at least one 'spiritual environmentalist':

> An awful lot of us just need to worship something. But in order to be able to worship, you have to be able to find something outside of yourself – and better than yourself. God is a construct for that. So is nature. We are falling in love with the environment as an extension to and in lieu of having fallen out of love with God. As it happens, it makes for a pretty deficient religion, but as an object of worship, nature takes some beating.[1]

But, according to Kaufman's definition, nature is an idol which has certain metaphysical implications. It leads us to believe that the reality we experience has no place for purpose, meaning or value. Contrast this with traditional western Christian metaphysics which asserts that ultimate reality is moral and personal.

For Kaufman this implies that orthodox Christianity cannot do more than give a secondary place to the impersonal aspects of creation. Conversely, to take 'nature' as we now understand it seriously will mean a radical re-examination of the Christian concept of God. A corollary of this is the impossibility of merely equating nature and the Christian concept of creation.

On the other hand, the apparent lack of purpose, meaning and value in nature causes Kaufman to doubt the value of a more naturalistic approach. He fears that the theological use of this concept may lead us to de-personalize a universe which Christianity regards as fundamentally personal.

In the end, Kaufman leaves us with questions rather than answers. He fails to offer us a middle path between a personalistic but anti-ecological theism and a de-personalizing naturalism. But is the dilemma as stark as he suggests?

It is worth noting that his definition of nature places too much weight on the purposelessness of nature. Purposeful activity is not the exclusive prerogative of the human species.

[1]Quoted in Porritt & Winner, 1988, pp. 251f.

It is true that strict philosophical naturalism demands the elimination of teleological explanation (*i.e.*, explanation in terms of final causes or purpose). However, we must distinguish between purposes and (ultimate) purpose. If Kaufman means that purposes are absent from nature, then he is simply wrong. If he means that nature lacks an ultimate purpose, then he is covertly assuming that human culture (in contrast to nature) possesses an ultimate purpose.

But, even if lack of purpose were implicit in the concept of nature, this would not, as Kaufman seems to suggest, preclude its use in Christian theology. Two quite different lines of theological reasoning may be cited in support of this contention.

First, purpose is by no means as central to Christian theology as Kaufman suggests. The machine analogy for creation, popular since the emergence of modern science, does indeed seem to require a purpose for creation. What is the machine for? But more recent theologies of creation which stress instead the analogy of artistic creation render such questions meaningless. We do not ask of a Mozart symphony, 'What is its purpose?'

Second, as Kaufman points out, theologians must always be on their guard when they make use of concepts from the culture in which they live. The meaning of terms used in Christian theology must be governed by the Christian revelation and not by their secular etymology. Kaufman has reminded us that nature may bear connotations which must be stripped away before the term may be used theologically. This is an important point to bear in mind in any re-examination of the Christian traditions for a theology of nature. However, to deny theologians the right to use (and, in using, to modify) the concept at all would be to undermine our attempts to respond to a major problem of our times.

4. Process theology

One contender in the race to reconstruct Christian theology along Green lines is process theology. Several of the most influential process theologians have publicly announced their commitment to the environmentalist cause. In addition, process thought (though not necessarily its theistic form) has been endorsed by a number of Deep Ecologists.

a. What is process theology?

Process theology is rooted in the work of British-born philosopher and mathematician, Alfred North Whitehead (1861–1947). He undertook a major revision of western metaphysics in the light of evolutionary thought and its emphasis on the temporality of our experience. To this end he sought to synthesize the two main strands of western metaphysical tradition, namely, the philosophies of Aristotle and Descartes.

In 1924 he accepted a post in the Philosophy Department at Harvard University. As a result his work has been far more influential in North America than in Europe. It was of particular interest to theologians because Whitehead found himself having to postulate the existence of something like God in order to maintain the internal coherence of his system. Thanks largely to the efforts of the philosophical theologian, Charles Hartshorne, process thought has become one of the major influences in contemporary American theological thought.

Fundamental to process theology is its understanding of reality. As the name suggests, it is about process: what is real is changing, active, becoming; it is in process. An unchanging entity is either dead or abstract – it is not real. The basic building block of reality is an actual entity – a momentary event of creative self-determination in response to preceding actual entities and the environment (including a pool of unrealized potentialities, eternal objects, forms, ideas, or universals). Everything is explicable in terms of actual entities.

This creates an unconventional perspective on every-day experience. You and I are not actual entities because we endure. In fact, even sub-atomic particles are not actual entities because they too endure! Such elementary particles may perhaps be thought of as a succession of actual entities in which a common characteristic is passed on from one to the next. Most ordinary physical objects can be analysed into many interrelated strands of such successions. Whitehead calls such objects, corpuscular societies.

What about living beings? According to Whitehead, life is a function of a special class of actual entity in which conceptual rather than physical feelings predominate. They constitute a vital agent dominating an otherwise inanimate object:

> Life is a characteristic of 'empty space' and not of space 'occupied' by any corpuscular society. . . . Life lurks in the interstices of each living cell, and in the interstices of the brain.[1]

Reality, if it is organized in this way, must be inherently social. There is a strong sense of interconnectedness in the way each entity is influenced by its predecessors and, in its turn, influences its successors. Everything is related to everything else.

Where does God enter into Whitehead's scheme? It appears that God must be invoked both to ensure the continuation and orderliness of natural process and to provide the ultimate basis for the appearance of novelty. However, for the sake of coherence, such a God cannot be understood as a transcendent creator. For Whitehead, he is one actual entity within the cosmos, albeit an entity with a unique function.

Most process theologians have gone well beyond Whitehead's rudimentary discussion of God. The majority follow Hartshorne in attempting to spell out how God can be both genuinely loving and ultimate within the constraints of process metaphysics. They are deeply dissatisfied with the classical philosophical model of God which presents a being whose very absoluteness seems to rule out the idea that God may be loving in any meaningful sense.

In contrast to the stress on divine unity in western philosophical theology, process theology suggests that God is dipolar. God is both necessary and contingent. The British process theologian David Pailin explains it thus:

> God's existence is uniquely to be understood as absolute, necessary and unchanging. God exists whatever else happens to be the case. There is no possible state which is not dependent upon him. At the same time the character of God's actuality is

[1]Whitehead, 1979, pp. 105f.

> determined partly by his own choices and partly by the actual states of the creation to which he is related as God – and so is relative, contingent and changing according to those choices and states.[1]

How is this dipolar God related to the world? A popular analogy amongst process theologians is that of the relationship between mind and body. They criticize traditional theism for so divorcing God and creation that they cannot be related in any meaningful way. Pantheism, on the other hand, fails because it makes it impossible to distinguish God and world. The mind-body analogy, however, suggests a being who is immediately related to every actual entity (just as a mind is related to the various parts of its associated body), but who is not simply identified with those parts (just as mind cannot be identified simply with changes of brain state). Alternatively, the relationship may be thought of as pan*en*theism: everything is *in* God.

b. Process thought and the environment

There are clear affinities between process thought and the worldviews of Deep Ecology. Process thought envisages nature as 'a dynamic process of becoming, always changing and developing, radically temporal in character'.[2] Furthermore, process thought recognizes the principle of interconnectedness which is so important to Green thought. According to Ian Barbour,

> it presents no dualism of body and soul and no sharp separation between the human and the non-human. Anthropocentrism is avoided because humanity is seen as part of the community of life and similar to other entities, despite distinctive human characteristics. All creatures are intrinsically valuable because each is a center of experience, though there are enormous gradations in the complexity and intensity of experience. In addition, by balancing immanence and transcendence, process thought encourages respect for nature.[3]

[1] *NDCT*, p. 469. [2] Barbour, 1990, p. 262. [3] *Ibid.*

Nevertheless, certain aspects of process thought render it an unlikely vehicle for a Green Christian spirituality. Most process thinkers adopt a rationalistic scholastic style which is very different from the poetic mystical style apparently favoured by the advocates of Green spirituality.

Nor are the differences merely a matter of style. In contrast to the radically holistic approach preferred by Greens, process thought tends to be reductionistic. Reality may be understood as an organic network of dynamic processes but those processes are not continuous. Whitehead proposed a radical quantization of reality when he insisted that 'The ultimate metaphysical truth is atomism. The creatures are atomic.'[1] Furthermore, these atomic actual entities are the only explanations in process thought – everything is explicable in terms of its fundamental building blocks: reductionism with a vengeance!

c. Implications for Christian theology

Nothing has so far been said about the distinctive features of Christian belief. This is because process theology is unashamedly a natural theology. The principles upon which its view of reality is based are derived not from revelation but from reason and scientific exploration of the cosmos. For process thinkers,

> The great virtue of Christianity has been that it is not so much a metaphysic seeking some historical grounding as it is an historical fact seeking for metaphysical explanation.[2]

In other words, the biblical traditions and the history of Christian thought and practice are no more than a collection of raw data awaiting analysis and interpretation within the framework of some metaphysical system.

The first casualty is the notion of divine action. Process thinkers insist that the process God cares for creation in a way which cannot be true of the God of classical theism. But at the same time they manage to rule out any meaningful concept

[1]Whitehead, 1979, p. 35.
[2]A. N. Whitehead quoted in Pittenger, 1968, p. 73.

of divine action. For process thought all events are to some extent divine acts. Any story which suggests that God really does act in space and time is treated as mythological. In fact, one influential process theologian even criticizes Bultmann for not taking his demythologizing far enough![1]

The mind-body analogy for the relationship between God and the world means that the Christian doctrine of creation from nothing must vanish. God and the universe are co-eternal.

The consistent reinterpretation of Christian doctrine in terms dictated by process philosophy can result only in the loss of Christianity's historical particularity; its distinctive basis for every-day living; and the rejection of its eschatological hope. Such a price is surely too high to pay merely to have a theology which enshrines the fundamental tenet of environmentalism.

5. Teilhard de Chardin

The writings of the Jesuit anthropologist Pierre Teilhard de Chardin are often classified as a form of process theology. However, he developed his system independently of A. N. Whitehead and, while there are similarities between them, the differences are so marked as to warrant separate treatment.

The environmental crisis has revived interest in Teilhard's views, particularly amongst his fellow Roman Catholics. Thus a number of Catholic theologians have used his work as the starting point for environmentalist theologies of nature.[2] He has also proved to be remarkably influential within the New Age movement: many of the present generation of New Age spokespersons cite his writings as one of the formative influences on their own thought.[3]

In spite of his unusual terminology, Teilhard's thought is far more orthodox than process theology. As a Catholic priest he simply was not exposed to the same philosophical

[1]Ogden, 1977, pp. 164–187. [2]*E.g.* Robert Faricy and Sean McDonagh.

[3]On the basis of a questionnaire sent to several hundred influential New Agers, Marilyn Ferguson cites Teilhard as the person most frequently mentioned as having influenced them (Ferguson, 1981, pp. 418–420).

and theological forces which shaped process thought. His training in theology occurred at a time when Thomism absolutely dominated Roman Catholic thought. Furthermore, for much of his life he was physically isolated from the theological and philosophical developments of Europe. Apart from traditional Roman Catholic doctrine, the main influences on his thinking were classical philosophy, the writings of the evolutionary philosopher Henri Bergson, and, above all, the evolutionary assumptions of modern biology and palaeontology.

a. Teilhard's evolutionary vision

Teilhard set himself the task of achieving a synthesis between Roman Catholic theology and evolutionary thought. In doing so he was following the example of St Thomas Aquinas rather than Hegel. He believed passionately in the unity of all knowledge (because of the unity of reality). It is often said that there are two books from which we can learn about God: the book of Scripture and the book of Nature. Teilhard insisted that both books tell the same story; that theology and modern science can and should be harmonized.

Like generations of natural theologians before him, Teilhard's starting point was the natural world and, as a biologist, specifically the concept of evolution. He set forth an evolutionary vision which could then be related to the traditional hierarchical metaphysics (and spirituality) of Roman Catholicism.

Initially the universe is chaotic: a flux of elementary particles in a state of maximum multiplicity and simplicity. However, God has implanted into these elements an urge towards unity and, thus, towards greater complexity and consciousness (the law of complexity-consciousness). All entities are dipolar: they possess both a 'without' (a degree of physical organization) and a 'within' (a degree of consciousness). Both dimensions evolve as simple entities combine together in increasingly complex structures.

The notion that a sub-atomic particle might have a rudimentary consciousness (a belief known as panpsychism) seems strange to many people. However, it is a consequence of Teilhard's adherence to belief in a Great Chain of Being. Nature does not proceed by leaps; everything occurs continuously and gradually. Consciousness clearly exists in humankind. Therefore it must have emerged gradually from some proto-consciousness.

Eventually, after billions of years, life emerged. A new phase in the evolution of the cosmos had begun: biogenesis. Gradually life covered the earth and gave rise to the biosphere. The emergence of life represented a quantum leap in the degree of complexity which could be achieved. The leading edge of evolution moved from the physical to the biological sphere.

The next significant phase was the emergence of animals with a central nervous system (Teilhard called it 'cephalization'). Again a quantum leap in evolution was possible with the first glimmerings of what we would recognize as consciousness.

This was followed, again after millions of years, by the emergence of the first humans – and fully functioning human consciousness ('noogenesis'). However, the twin drives towards greater complexity and greater consciousness continue. The human race expands to fill the earth ('planetization') while, at the same time, human cultures become more sophisticated and gradually merge ('convergence'). In Teilhard's opinion, the twentieth century marked the probable limits of this phase of evolution.

b. From evolution to theology

From the beginning, all of creation has been striving towards God. The dual thrust of planetization and convergence represents the final phase before the achievement of that goal. This is the point at which Teilhard explicitly reverts to Christian theology and it becomes apparent that his entire evolutionary vision has been set up with just this goal in mind.

The emergence of planetary consciousness (which he sees as the next step forward) is identified as the Omega Point: the emergence of the glorified Christ. The church is in a literal sense the body of Christ;[1] the seed of the cosmic Christ planted in the evolutionary process. As the transition to the

[1]Teilhard reveals himself to be a true son of Rome in suggesting that the Roman Catholic Church (and, particularly, the Pope) is the central nervous system of the body of Christ! See Santmire, 1985, p. 164.

next phase of evolution occurs, that seed will grow and blossom into the body of Christ-Omega.

The glorified, fulfilled Christ is the heart, the meaning and the consummation of the evolutionary process. He is the final cause of the universe, drawing all things to himself by the force of love.

This leads to a very real eschatology. Paul Santmire describes it thus:

> When Christ does reach his own fullness, his highly intensified, infinitely spiritualized body will be the only surviving reality. Biophysical reality generally will die a death of heatlessness and will disintegrate toward nothingness. But human reality will be transfigured into the white heat of ultimate charity, in the fullness of Christ. The members of the mystical body will then be united once and for all to the head. ... The cosmic ascent of humanity will have reached its final goal, union with the universal Christ, and through him, union with God, who will then be all in all.[1]

We would do well to investigate Teilhard's understanding of the cosmic Christ a little more closely. The concept of the cosmic Christ is fundamental to the biblical understanding of Christ (*e.g.* Col. 1:15–20) but, in recent years, it has frequently been divorced from the historical Jesus. Many theosophical and New Age writers do this, using 'Christ' to refer to an immanent spiritual force which may be incarnated in human beings (Jesus is usually regarded as one such incarnation or *avatar*, along with Buddha and many other 'masters of wisdom').

The same cannot be said of Teilhard. He makes it quite clear that the historical Jesus and the cosmic Christ are uniquely related. Commenting on the fundamentals of Christian belief, he remarks that 'Faith in the divinity of the historical Christ (not only as prophet and perfect man, but as an object also of love and worship)' is essential.[2] A genuine incarnation of God in space-time is an essential part of

[1]Santmire, 1985, p. 164. [2]Teilhard, 1974, p. 94.

Teilhard's vision since that is the foundation upon which the church is built. The life, death and resurrection of Jesus Christ enable people to become part of a new community, a new organism: the body of Christ.

c. Nature in Teilhard's thought

The language may be new but the vision is that of Christian Platonism. Unlike most contemporary advocates of the principle of interconnectedness, Teilhard has retained the hierarchical aspect of the Great Chain of Being. His predecessors, such as St Bonaventure, believed that meditation on the footprints (or vestiges) of God in nature (not least the Chain of Being) was one important way in which the human soul ascends to God. For them, nature was a ladder reaching up to God. But when the ascent was complete they could kick the ladder away; nature and the material creation were of no further significance.

Teilhard loved the natural world and gave it a much greater place in his thought than many earlier theologians. Darwinism had temporalized the Chain of Being. Thus, the evolutionary process itself could become, for Teilhard, the means by which humankind ascends to God. However, nature remains strictly secondary in his vision. What really matters to him is that portion of the material world which is humanity. Even there, the inward, spiritual pole is infinitely more important than the outward, physical pole. For Teilhard, evolution is characterized by the emergence and ultimate dominance of the spiritual dimension of reality while the physical dimension withers away.[1] Like the Christian Platonists of the Middle Ages he was content to kick the ladder away when the ascent was complete.

This is a theology of nature which remains rooted in the western Christian tradition (albeit, a strand of that tradition which will not commend itself to many evangelicals). However, it is only superficially a Green theology. Teilhard's retention of a hierarchical understanding of reality completely undermines the Green potential of his theology.

[1]*E.g.* Teilhard, 1965, pp. 315f.; see also Mooney, 1968, pp. 196–198; Santmire, 1985, pp. 155–171, pp. 254–257.

6. Creation spirituality

This is a popular movement inspired by an American Dominican priest, Matthew Fox.[1] Fox's interest in developing a green spirituality dates back to his doctoral studies in Paris where he sat at the feet of M. D. Chenu, a distinguished Roman Catholic church historian. It took on a feminist/liberation theology dimension as a result of teaching in an American women's college. In 1977 he founded the Institute in Culture and Creation Spirituality. The faculty of that Institute give some indication of the eclecticism of Fox's approach: it includes the Wiccan priestess Starhawk, Luisah Teish (a Voudun priestess), Buck Ghost Horse (a Native American medicine man) and an Episcopalian priest turned Zen Buddhist!

Unlike either of the preceding candidates for a Green Christian theology, the emphasis of creation spirituality is largely practical and experiential. Thus it is much more accessible to the average layman. It has also achieved a certain curiosity value, not to say notoriety, since 1984 when Fox came to the attention of the Sacred Congregation for the Doctrine of the Faith (formerly the Holy Office of the Inquistion). At present he remains under investigation.

a. The four paths

Fox invites us to embark upon a pilgrimage along four spiritual paths which he describes as befriending creation; befriending darkness; befriending creativity; and befriending new creation.

He claims that these paths represent the spiritual tradition of Jesus himself: a tradition which has consistently been suppressed by the institutional church. Reclaiming this tradition for contemporary Christianity will, he promises, open up new possibilities for the solution not only of deep rifts within the Christian faith but also for global problems of social justice and ecology.

i. Befriending creation is presented as a counter-balance to what he perceives as the church's dualistic hatred of the material world and its corollary, asceticism. He calls on us to

[1]His ideas are set out in great detail in Fox, 1983.

see creation as a blessing rather than a curse. It is God's gift to us, to be enjoyed; not a prison which separates the soul from God.

ii. Befriending darkness is very similar to the *via negativa* of traditional Christian spirituality. It involves the giving up of our images and words to find God in silence and the luminous darkness of Christian mysticism.

But it also involves the acceptance of pain. By working through our pain instead of suppressing it we become more sensitive to the pain of others, both human and non-human. Pain burns away false pleasures; enables us to endure; creates bonds of compassion. For Fox, this is the way of the Cross.

iii. Befriending creativity moves us on to a more active spirituality. Like so many Christians today, Fox identifies our creativity with the divine image in us. Thus he also calls this path, 'befriending our divinity'. He recommends artistic activity as a form of meditation. Nor is it limited to what is conventionally understood as art; our whole lives are to be seen as works of art, beautifying God's good creation.

iv. Befriending new creation is the fourth and last stage of Fox's plan. Like the previous stage it is active. It calls upon us to look outwards to the world. It calls upon us to work out our Christian faith in the very practical activity of seeking personal, social and ecological justice.

b. The underlying theology

On the face of it, Fox offers us an attractive spirituality. He rightly turns away from the tendency to despise the body which has been prevalent in western spirituality. Similarly, his insistence on linking spirituality with the way we live and relate to others is a valuable corrective to the tendency to view spirituality as something private, entirely between the individual and God. However, as we shall see, all that glitters is not gold.

Fox clearly identifies creation with nature and, as we saw in section 3, p. 64, this must entail a radical revision of our understanding of God. The route taken by Fox is to espouse panentheism. Again he is motivated by a desire to root out dualism (which he sees in the classical theistic contrast between Creator and creation).

In using this concept he hopes to avoid the heresy of

pantheism. However, the symbolism he adopts for speaking about God is overwhelmingly horizontal. Panentheism claims to maintain God's transcendence along with a greater stress on his immanence. But Fox's manner of speaking about God fails to do justice to that transcendence. The impression is that God is to be sought within (within the world, within the human unconscious) rather than through the world. There is little or no sense that God is beyond the world.

The radical immanence of God is also implicit in Fox's understanding of *dabhar*, divine creative energy, or 'original blessing'. This energy infuses all of creation. It flows through everything, uniting creatures with one another and with their divine ground. Fox variously describes this energy as the power of fertility and the desire behind creation. He even goes so far as to identify it with *eros* (the cosmic force which, in Hellenistic thought, causes the multiplicity of creation to strive after divine unity). As one would expect, Fox adheres to the principle of interconnectedness and even celebrates its monistic tendencies.

Just how important this concept is to Fox is clear from the way he allows it to transform his understanding of the relationship between God and creation (particularly human creatures). Since divine energy flows through all things and is the reality of which words are merely symbolic, 'We are part of that flow and we need to listen to it rather than to assume arrogantly that our puny words are the only words of God.'[1] By 'our puny words' he means the Judaeo-Christian Scriptures (and, indeed, the scriptures of every other religion). Since God's energy is prior to mere words, creation must take priority over revelation as the source of our theology and spirituality.

A corollary of this is that the path to God begins with an ecstatic immersion in creation. In this way, 'We become like the Creator and take on the Creator's characteristics.'[2] This suggests that Fox's revision of Christian theology must extend to his concept of salvation.

Salvation, for Fox, is emphatically not a process of being redeemed from a fallen state. He rejects the whole edifice of fall/redemption spirituality and theology as fundamental to

[1]Fox, 1983, pp. 38f. [2]Fox, 1981, p. 79.

the dualism he seeks to overcome. Indeed, for Fox, a fall/redemption mentality is the very root of sin, leading, in his view, to 'sexism, militarism, racism, genocide against native peoples, biocide, consumerist capitalism, and violent communism'.[1]

On the contrary, we need to be saved from our enslavement to the notion of fall and redemption. This salvation is achieved by the awakening of *eros*. As our desire for unity is brought to life by the exploration of sexuality, the arts, dance, *t'ai chi*, yoga, shamanistic rituals, or any of the myriad consciousness-altering techniques currently available, we begin to experience our oneness. We overcome all the pernicious dualities of western thought. The distinctions between body and soul, man and woman, human and non-human, creature and God are dissolved.

Fox's rhetoric is clearly designed to appeal to those who are in sympathy with New Age thinking rather than traditional Christianity. Speaking of the contemporary explosion of New Consciousness, he comments that, 'If entire religious bodies such as Christianity could enter into this expanding spiritual energy field, there is no predicting what powers of passion and compassion might become unleashed.'[2]

At the same time he launches a vitriolic attack on Augustine's influence on western Christianity. He presents a gross oversimplification and distortion of the relationship between fall/redemption spirituality and creation spirituality within western Christianity. The very theologians he celebrates as representatives of the minority creation tradition (*e.g.* Hildegard of Bingen) were also staunch advocates of fall/redemption spirituality. A more accurate view would be that the two have co-existed in tension with one another. It is when one or other of the two traditions has been suppressed that the church has lurched towards heresy. One is left with the uneasy feeling that this is not so much Christian spirituality as New Age thought in Christian trappings.

[1]Fox, 1983, pp. 28f. [2]*Ibid.*, p. 315.

7. Conclusion: difficulties with panentheism

Both process theology and Matthew Fox's creation spirituality adopt a panentheistic view of God. Both suggest that a model of God's relationship to the world, based on the analogy of the relationship between mind and body, is to be preferred over the alternatives. In my opinion, Teilhard does not go down the same road. He retains an essentially orthodox view of God, simply putting much greater emphasis on the processes of creation than earlier theologies. However, as we have seen, to the extent that this conservative reading of Teilhard is accurate, he fails to come up with a satisfactory Green theology of nature.

Gordon Kaufman, whose concerns we examined earlier in this chapter, has pointed out that our view of nature (or creation) and our understanding of God are inextricably linked. In the interests of maintaining an ecocentric perspective on the natural world, many Green theologians have modified their view of God towards panentheism. However, this raises a number of problems for anyone who also wants to maintain an orthodox Christian faith.

To begin with, there are problems with the analogy itself. It seems initially attractive to say God is related to world as mind is to body. But just how is mind related to body? The relationship between mind and body is one of the intractable problems of western philosophy. In using the mind/body analogy we effectively transpose that problem into theology. Clearly those who use the analogy will not be satisfied with the dualistic solution.

What about the view that one is merely an artefact of the other? The materialist form of this solution would deny the ultimate reality of mind and God. The idealist form would deny the reality of body and world. Neither is particularly satisfactory!

Perhaps mind and body are co-equal, different aspects of the one reality. But applying this to God and the world results in pantheism.

Quite apart from the difficulties within the analogy itself, panentheism raises serious problems for a Christian understanding of creation. *Creatio ex nihilo* would seem to indicate that God (mind) is prior to creation (body). Can we maintain a Christian doctrine of creation with such an analogy? The panentheist response may well be to point to that strand of Christian tradition which regarded God as essentially creative.[1] If creativity is essential to God then God and his creative activity must be co-eternal. But this rapidly leads to the divinization of the world. Again panentheism slides towards pantheism.

If panentheism is not an option, are there untapped resources within the orthodox doctrine of God which would allow us to respond positively to the environmental crisis? This question will be picked up again in chapter 6 after we have reviewed the biblical traditions regarding the natural world in the next chapter.

[1]The clearest example would be the Greek Father, Origen.

CHAPTER FIVE

Nature in the Bible

1. Pre-understanding and word-blindness

No book, not even the Bible, can be read *de novo*. Whenever we begin to read we bring some pre-understanding to the text; we rely upon a tradition of interpretation to make sense of what we read. We make assumptions about the meanings of words and phrases, about the sorts of questions the text will tackle, and even about the desired answers to those questions.

It might appear that reading can only confirm our own prejudices. However, I do not believe that such a pessimistic judgment is justified. What it does mean is that *uncritical* reading of any book is as likely to confirm your own prejudices as to bring you fresh insights. Responsible reading is self-critical; it entails examining your own prejudices and presuppositions as you read. The hallmark of responsible reading is a willingness to be questioned by the text even as you question it. Responsible reading is a dialogue between the author and reader; it permits the text to maintain its integrity. Or, as one literary critic puts it; 'A book will never draw me out of myself if I only accept as belonging to it what I have already decreed should be there.'[1]

How does this apply to the Bible's understanding of the natural world? Lynn White castigates the biblical account of creation for divorcing the human race from nature (linking us to God through the notion of the image of God) and setting us over nature (through the notion of dominion). Furthermore, it is possible to find ample support for his views in the writings of Bible commentators and expositors. In fact, anthropocentric interpretations of the biblical accounts of creation have been almost universal amongst recent generations of theologians. The question which must be asked is whether this is justified by the text itself or has been read into it by unconscious accommodation to prevailing cultural assumptions.

One point at which anthropocentric assumptions become visible is in the historical–critical interpretation of biblical creation accounts. Alongside its analytical approach to the text, historical criticism often assumes that the results of its analysis must be interpreted in an evolutionary manner, with the earliest texts assumed to represent the creative phase of Hebrew theology. As a result, effort tends to be concentrated on these early texts at the expense of later ones.

Unfortunately, the most important biblical creation texts are usually regarded as late. This has had the effect of playing down the importance of creation within the Bible. Thus, one of the 'assured results' of Old Testament studies is that the earliest Hebrews were not conscious of the cosmic scope of God's activity. They were aware only of their personal and national dependence on Yahweh. Biblical creation material is dismissed as secondary and creation itself is regarded as a mere backdrop for the drama of salvation-history: it is assumed that the biblical authors intended to collapse creation into soteriology. John Reumann concludes that,

> God's creative work, while involving the whole world, is especially understood in the Bible to affect men. ... Thus, whether creation is thought of as initial creation at the beginning, continuing

[1]Josipovici, 1988, p. 15.

> creation, or future creation, the formulations in the Bible have an *anthropological or existential thrust.* Man and his existence are the concern.[1]

Anthropocentric interpretations of creation are by no means new. However, the anthropological importance of the biblical accounts has been stressed almost to the exclusion of other dimensions by the impact of philosophical existentialism on twentieth-century theology.

It seems likely that the combined effect of existential and evolutionary assumptions would be to exaggerate the anthropological dimensions of the text. Thus, in re-examining biblical attitudes to nature in the light of the environmental crisis, we must ask ourselves whether the texts in question are as anthropocentric as has usually been assumed.

2. Old Testament perspectives

a. The primeval history

Whatever their prehistory, the present form and location of these chapters clearly contradict any interpretation merely in terms of human salvation. Far from being just an explanation of Israel's origins, they place both the Hebrew and Christian traditions firmly in a cosmic context. From the outset, the God who brought Hebrew slaves out of Egypt and created from them the nation of Israel, who revealed himself in Jesus Christ and who acted decisively to overcome human sin through Jesus' death and resurrection, is presented as the Creator of the entire universe. By reporting the origin, not only of the church and Israel, but of the universe as a whole, the primeval history reminds us that the scope of divine activity is more than enough to encompass salvation history. There can be no question of restricting its scope to specifically salvific events. On the contrary, it must be taken to include *all* things and events.

i. Creation from nothing?: There has been much debate about whether Genesis 1 supports the Christian doctrine of

[1]Reumann, 1973, p. 68.

creatio ex nihilo or a doctrine of divine ordering of a primordial chaos. At present the majority of Old Testament scholars favour the former interpretation, taking verse 1 as a principal sentence prefixed to the chapter as a whole.[1] Thus the first verse of the Bible makes an assertion quite unprecedented in ancient near-eastern literature: it ascribes the entire work of creation exclusively to the one God.

Nevertheless, the Genesis account is less than explicit, with its description of the primordial earth as 'formless and empty' (Gn. 1:2). There is still scope for interpreting these verses as speaking of uncreated raw material. A theological argument against this interpretation will be advanced in the next chapter.

Meanwhile, assuming the traditional Christian doctrine of creation, this verse is most probably speaking of raw material *created* by God as the first stage in the process of creation. Its significance for a theology of nature is that even the humblest matter is an integral (indeed, a fundamental) part of God's good creation. There is no suggestion in Genesis 1 of the sinister overtones which sometimes attach to formlessness and void elsewhere in the Old Testament.[2]

ii. Creation as a speech-act: At eight points in Genesis 1 God speaks creatively: 'And God said, "Let . . ."' (verses 3, 6, 9, 11, 14, 20, 24 and 26). This use of speech as a metaphor for the divine activity of creation suggests something voluntary, effortless and rational.

It follows that creaturely existence is to be understood as the appropriate response to the divine word. But what sort of speech-act and response are envisaged here? Different answers to this question will result in different understandings of the God–world relationship.

It is undeniable that the speech formulae of Genesis 1 take the form of commands and their fulfilment. The fact that no-one is addressed is sometimes taken to mean that the act of creation was magical.[3] However, words of magic are essentially ahistorical: they belong to the realm of mythology. Such an interpretation of the creative speech of Genesis 1 is possible only by ignoring its context as the preface to a history.

[1]Westermann, 1984, pp. 94–97.
[2]*E.g.* Dt. 32:10; Jb. 6:18; 12:24; Is. 24:10; 34:11; 40:23; Je. 4:23.
[3]*E.g.* Cupitt, 1990, p. 8.

God's word of command in creation operates effortlessly in obtaining what it has defined. But this is not magic, for it is continuous with his words of command spoken in human history.

However, the divine creative commands need to be contrasted with what we usually understand as commands. There is an element of openness which distinguishes them from the notion of specific obligation normally implied by the word 'command'. True, the creative commands set limits upon creaturely existence – they impose order upon the formlessness and void. But, at the same time, they hold out the possibility of tremendous variety in the unfolding of creation within those limits.

Thus, while recognizing the command and execution structure of Genesis 1, we must not allow this to mislead us into thinking that God's creative activity is narrowly deterministic. On the contrary, in uttering those commands, 'God gives permission for creation to be. The appearance of creation is a glad act of embrace of this permit.'[1] More positively, the creative words may be regarded as holding out a promise to creation, as offering created being the gift of a future with God.[2]

iii. The de-divinization of nature: Christianity is often accused of de-divinizing nature. That this is, in fact, the case is quite clear from these chapters. Indeed Genesis 1 has been described as a polemic against ancient near-eastern nature cults.

Three examples of this attack on the divinity of nature may be cited from Genesis 1. First, Genesis 1:2 demotes the primordial chaos from its status as the actively aggressive matrix of the gods to that of mere (divinely created) raw material for the categories of existence. Second, the account of the fourth day of creation is unusually repetitive. It takes particular pains to stress the human utility of the sun, moon and stars. This is not anthropocentrism but an attack upon the astral cults which were so important to Israel's neighbours. Third, God's blessing of creation implies a denial of the divinity of nature: fertility is not a capacity of an autonomous nature but remains the gift of God the Creator.

[1]Brueggemann, 1982, p. 30. [2]Jenson, 1973, p. 7.

iv. The goodness of nature and the divine blessing: Seven times in Genesis 1 God declares creation to be good. It is striking that non-human creatures are unequivocally stated to be good without reference to humankind. However, this does not mean that creatures are good in themselves. Goodness is not presented as an attribute of creatures either individually or as a whole. Rather, it is a divine judgment about creation carrying both moral and aesthetic overtones. This assessment does not result from detached contemplation but from active engagement with the creature. The creature is good (and, hence, beautiful) by virtue of its standing in appropriate relationship to its creator.

The divine blessing is reserved until the fifth and sixth days of creation where it is applied first to birds and sea creatures and then to humankind. We are told also that God blessed and hallowed the seventh day. This blessing is a granting of the power to be fruitful and multiply.[1]

v. The status of humankind: Traditional readings of the primeval history stress the special status it appears to confer on humankind. The creation of humankind is seen as the climax of Genesis 1, and this is reinforced by the prior creation of Adam in Genesis 2. God appears to give us a special blessing; we are portrayed as made in the image of God (in contrast to other creatures); and we are given a dominion over the other creatures which is shown to have disastrous implications for them in the flood story.

The primeval history clearly distinguishes and elevates humankind over the rest of creation. However, several features also stress the intimacy of the relationship between humans and the non-human creation.

First, humankind is created on the same day as the land animals: suggesting a certain kinship. Second, it is simply wrong to regard the creation of humankind as the climax of Genesis 1: that privilege is accorded not to humankind, but to the establishment of God's Sabbath communion with creation as a whole. Third, the very fact that the creation of humankind appears in the same passage as the creation of the non-human, contrasts with the ancient near-eastern tendency to separate accounts of cosmic and human origins.

[1]Westermann, 1974, pp. 139f.

Finally, it is not clear that the divine blessing of verse 28a by itself distinguishes humans from the non-human. God has already pronounced a similar blessing upon sea creatures and birds (verse 22), and it is arguable that the blessing of verse 28a is actually inclusive of the land animals created in verses 24 and 25.[1]

This impression of interdependence is further reinforced by the more detailed account of the creation of humankind in Genesis 2. Adam is placed in the garden in order to maintain it. The primeval history also bears witness to the negative implications of this interdependence: human sin results in the 'de-creation' of the flood.

vi. The nature of dominion: The command to have dominion is closely related to the divine blessing: 'Be fruitful and increase in number; fill the earth and subdue it. Rule over the fish of the sea and the birds of the air and over every living creature that moves on the ground' (Gn. 1:28).

As I pointed out in chapter 2, Lynn White and others suggest that this command mandates us to trample nature underfoot. However, this is not a *carte blanche* to exploit the environment. The human race is permitted to subdue the earth, but this is a warrant for agriculture and nothing more. We are given the fruit of the earth to be our food. Dominion in Genesis 1 does not extend to the killing of animals for food (or clothing).

These considerations rule out the use of this text to justify an adversarial view of humankind's relation to the environment. On the contrary, this command transforms the blessing, at least as far as humankind is concerned, into a divine vocation. And that vocation to dominion over nature must be interpreted in terms of the concept of kingship familiar to the ancient Israelites. As I pointed out in chapter 2, such a ruler exists *for* his subjects.[2]

This understanding of dominion is reinforced by Genesis 2. Again the common origin of humankind and animals is pointed out. Indeed, our sheer physicality is celebrated here. Thus, in his commentary on Genesis 1 – 3, Bonhoeffer argues that our very embodiment should remind us of our

[1]Westermann, 1984, p. 160. [2]Westermann, 1974, p. 52.

relationship to the earth, to the non-human creation.[1]

Genesis 2 expands on the call to have dominion in two respects: Adam is called to till and keep the garden; and he is invited by God to name the animals.

Significantly, Genesis 1 presents God as refraining from naming the specific creatures created on and after the third day. The act of naming was an expression of ownership or sovereignty. God expresses his sovereignty over all creation by naming the basic categories of created existence. However, God graciously devolves upon the human race the privilege and responsibility of naming the particular creatures. Naming them is a demonstration of human dominion. Adam is ordering his world, incorporating the animals into his life. It is also a demonstration of human insight and wisdom.[2]

Lest this be interpreted as the first step on the road to the exploitation of nature, the context of this act should be recalled. The naming occurs in the presence of God (thus relativizing any claim to human sovereignty) and it arises from the search for a suitable partner for Adam. No animal was suitable, but the entertainment of the possibility bears witness to a positive relation to the non-human.

vii. The environmental implications of human disobedience: Adam's disobedience in Genesis 3 and its ecological consequences highlight the ambivalence of nature that was experienced by the Hebrews (and which is shared by country people to this day). It is to be received gladly as a gift of God, but it is also a place of thorns and thistles, of stinging insects and predatory animals. Above all, it threatens us with personal extinction through disease and natural disaster. Remarkably, this ambivalence is explained not in terms of the recalcitrance of matter but in terms of human disobedience. The disobedience of Adam consisted in his rejection of the divine boundaries placed upon his dominion of the earth. It was a rebellion against the good order of creation established by God in Genesis 1.

The result, expressed in terms of divine judgment, is the disruption of the relationships established by God (specifically between God and humankind, between man and woman, and humankind and other creatures). Adam no

[1]Bonhoeffer, 1959, p. 46. [2]Blocher, 1984, p. 91.

longer has a harmonious relationship with God, Eve, or nature: he has lost his dominion over the earth. Furthermore, there is no way in which he can regain that dominion for himself: he is barred from Eden by the cherubim.

The environmental implications of human disobedience are further highlighted by the flood narrative. It portrays a world in which the vocation of humankind to be stewards of creation has been supplanted by the quest for autonomy. This quest is characterized by the spread of human violence. However, the unique status of humankind means that this violence corrupts the whole of creation.

Since humans have denied the good order of creation in their quest for self-deification, the form of judgment is appropriately a temporary suspension of that order. There is a virtual return to the initial 'waste and void' brought about by the temporary withdrawal of the active divine care implicit in Genesis 1.

At the same time, the faithful Noah is called to exercise human dominion over creation precisely in the preservation of representative animals from the judgment that is about to overwhelm the world. Noah's family, *together with the animals* in the ark (Gn. 8:1), constitute the first appearance of that *leitmotif* of the Old Testament, the faithful remnant.

The present environmental crisis may be regarded as a contemporary expression of the disruption of our relationship with the environment brought about by human disobedience.[1] In this connection it is worth recalling Bonhoeffer's judgment on western technology. He argued that technology was fallen humankind's substitute for God's gift of dominion. However, as the story of Babel makes clear, far from being our key to mastery over nature, our fellow men and ultimately God himself, it is the agent of our enslavement and destruction:

> Technology is the power with which the earth grips man and subdues him. . . . We do not rule because we do not know the world as God's creation, and because we do not receive our dominion as God-given but grasp it for ourselves. There is no

[1]Steck, 1980, p. 75.

'being-free-from' without 'being-free-for'. There is no dominion without serving God. . . . Without God, without his brother, man loses the earth.[1]

viii. A covenant with nature: The flood narrative concludes with the establishment of an everlasting covenant between God and the inhabitants of the ark: Noah and his descendants and *every* living creature. Covenants which include the non-human are a recurring theme in the Old Testament, particularly amongst the prophets (*e.g.* Ho. 2:18; Je. 33:20–25; Ezk. 34:25). It is symptomatic of the pervasive anthropocentrism of our culture that so many commentators simply overlook this fact.

What is the content of this covenant? Dumbrell reminds us that 'covenants presupposed a set of existing relationships to which by formal ceremony they gave binding expression'.[2] Here the relationships which receive formal expression are those which endured through the flood, including Noah's care for the animals. The wording of the covenant recalls the divine blessing of chapter 1. But, in addition to the blessing, God now gives an unconditional promise to maintain for all time the basic conditions of order which are a precondition for being able to respond to the blessing.

The Noahic Covenant institutionalizes humankind's alienation from nature by granting us permission to eat flesh. However, it does not constitute a charter to exploit the non-human. On the contrary, the divine prohibition on the drinking of blood may be taken as a reminder that humankind has not been given arbitrary power over other living creatures.[3]

Finally, it should be noted that the issues raised in the primeval history are not settled there. The reality of human violence and the ambivalence of nature carry forward into the patriarchal history and, thence, to the present. What the primeval history leaves us with is the promise residing in the covenant with Noah. The covenant has redemptive implications which concern not only humankind but the whole of God's creation. It is an everlasting covenant with the

[1]Bonhoeffer, 1959, p. 38. [2]Dumbrell, 1984, p. 20.
[3]Gowan, 1987, p. 104.

non-human as well. The clear implication is that the final consummation of all things concerns the non-human as well as the human.

b. Nature elsewhere in the Pentateuch and historical books

It is true that the primeval history strikes a rather different note from subsequent chapters and books. Only Genesis 1 – 11 speaks explicitly about the place of the non-human in God's scheme of things. Thus it is tempting for those who accept the critical consensus to regard these chapters as a cosmic prologue cobbled on to an essentially anthropocentric tradition at a late date.

However, it is very easy to overstress this contrast. If we read the historical books of the Old Testament with a sensitivity to references to the non-human we shall find that they are less anthropocentric than first impressions might suggest.

i. Nature in Old Testament law: There are relatively few references to the non-human dimensions of creation in Old Testament law. However, they make interesting reading.

Since ancient Israel was a predominantly agrarian society it is not surprising that most of these regulations have to do with agriculture. Taken together, they amount to a ban on exploitative agricultural methods: intercropping to increase yields is forbidden (Lv. 19:19); fruit trees are not to be harvested until they are well established (Lv. 19:23–25); and the land is to be allowed to lie fallow during the sabbatical year (Ex. 23:10–11).

While these regulations may be given a utilitarian gloss, the same cannot be said of others. Thus domestic animals are to be permitted to rest on the Sabbath (Ex. 20:8–11; 23:12); and oxen are not to be muzzled when they tread out grain (Dt. 25:4). Furthermore, the animals belonging to an enemy are to be treated with similar respect (Ex. 23:4–5). It is hard to avoid the conclusion that domestic animals are considered to be more than mere chattels.

ii. Nature and the temple: The various traditions concerning the Jerusalem temple make interesting reading in this context. Certain elements in its construction may be seen as iconic of Eden. Of course, care must be taken not to read too much into these features: the history of biblical interpretation is littered with the most lurid speculation (*e.g.* reading astrological symbolism into the numbers of candelabra). Nevertheless, it is worth dwelling briefly on the references to nature in the relevant texts.

The tabernacle and the temple which succeeded it were not starkly functional sanctuaries. They bore little resemblance to the bare and ugly interiors of too many modern churches. On the contrary, they were highly decorated 'with representations of nature, flowers, blossoms, things of natural beauty'.[1] Exodus 25:31–33 refers to candlesticks fashioned like almond blossoms. The pillars of the temple were decorated with pomegranates (2 Ch. 3:16–17). The great bath before the altar (itself possibly a reference to a primordial sea) rested upon statues of oxen and was shaped like a lily (2 Ch. 4:3–5). And the walls of the temple were covered in bas-reliefs of flowers, trees and animals (1 Ki. 6:29; 7:29). As if this were not enough, 'when the priest went into the Holy of Holies, he was to take with him on his garments a representation of nature, carrying that representation into the presence of God'[2] (Ex. 28:33).

My point is simply that, in constructing a place of worship, the Israelites built in to it reminders of the natural world. Even in the Holy of Holies, the presence of God, they would have representations of nature before them. This was surely not because nature was for them an object of worship but, rather, because it was their first meeting place with God. The temple of Adam was the Garden of Eden itself.

c. *Nature in the worship of Israel*

Reference to the temple naturally leads us to look at Israel's worship and, in particular, the book of Psalms. Here we find considerable use being made of creation and nature imagery.

In many places the imagery is used in the service of other theological themes, in particular, the creation of Israel and the maintenance of the social order (*e.g.* Pss. 74:13–17; 77:16–20). However, their use of creation is never mere imagery. It is clear from the Israelite Wisdom tradition that the psalmists and those who used their poetry in worship would have recognized a genuine correspondence between the cosmic order and the social order. Thus their references

[1] F. Schaeffer, 1973, p. 13. [2] *Ibid.*, p. 14.

to creation were not merely expressive. God's covenantal care for Israel had real material and ecological implications. Conversely, God's continuing care for his creation had implications for the social and political order. But belief in the latter rested upon belief in the former.

A number of psalms are distinguished by their concentration on the divine creative activity (past and present). Amongst the biblical passages often regarded as creation psalms are Psalms 8; 19:1–6; 104; 139; 148; and outside the Psalter, Amos 4:13; 5:8–9; 9:5–6; and Job 38 – 41.

i. Psalm 104: Outstanding among the creation psalms is Psalm 104. It is unique in its exclusive use of God's creative activity as a basis for praise. Surely here is a passage which gives the lie to the contention that the biblical creation traditions are incorrigibly anthropocentric.

Unfortunately, the anthropocentric reading of biblical creation passages is so well established that Psalm 104 is often dismissed as an alien intrusion into the Psalter.[1] However, this overlooks that the psalm is clearly continuous with the Old Testament Wisdom tradition. The nearest biblical parallel is the divine challenge which forms the climax of the book of Job (Jb. 38 – 41). A negative judgment on Psalm 104 implies a similar judgment on the entire corpus of Wisdom literature in the Old Testament.[2] Furthermore, the psalm displays a clear affinity with the account of creation in the first chapter of Genesis.[3]

Psalm 104 does strike a rather different note to that of the primeval history when it refers to humankind. Unlike the other creatures, God's provision for us is not immediate: God supplies the plants but we must cultivate them. Thus we are given an element of responsibility withheld from other creatures. However, apart from this distinction, we are seen as entirely one with the animal kingdom in our dependence on God. The reason for this difference of emphasis is probably that it enables the psalmist to put greater emphasis on the present sustaining activity of God. The context of praise

[1]It is often compared with an Egyptian hymn to the Sun composed in the fourteenth century BC.

[2]Just such a judgment is often made by the critical consensus, *e.g.* Zimmerli, 1964, pp. 146–158.

[3]Kidner, 1975, p. 368.

makes it inappropriate for him to draw attention away from God's activity by stressing human dominion. Nevertheless, it complements rather than contradicts what the primeval history has to say about dominion.

d. Nature in the prophetic tradition

The critical tendency to regard the themes of creation and divine activity in nature as relatively late has also had its effect on readings of the prophetic tradition. Specifically, they are regarded as marks of post-exilic prophecy. Where explicit creation passages appear in texts which are indisputably pre-exilic, those passages are seen as later additions. If we relax the presupposition that creation is a late and marginal theme, a rather different picture is forthcoming.

Three themes are particularly relevant to the present study:

i. Judgment and the reversal of creation: I have already commented on this in connection with the flood narrative. It is particularly prominent amongst the pre-exilic prophets. Yahweh is presented as revoking or suspending the harmonious order of creation as an act of judgment upon a faithless Israel. This usage reflects the Wisdom tradition of a correspondence between the moral and the natural: disharmony in the former is presented as having serious consequences for the latter.

A stark example of this is Isaiah 24:1–13. The prophet envisages the judgment of the Lord in terms of an ecological catastrophe. Similarly Hosea presents a picture of desolation as a direct consequence of human sinfulness: 'Because of this the land mourns, and all who live in it waste away: the beasts of the field and the birds of the air and the fish of the sea are dying' (Ho. 4:3). The same theme appears in Zephaniah and frequently in Jeremiah.

ii. The covenant with nature: According to the conventional wisdom, the pre-exilic prophets are overwhelmingly judgmental. However, there is a positive strand in their use of nature and creation themes. Like the reversal of creation, it is a theme which we have already noted in the flood narrative.

Judgment does not result in final destruction. On the contrary, a faithful remnant will be preserved. And, says Yahweh to that remnant, 'I will make for you a covenant on that day with the beasts of the field, the birds of the air, and the creeping things of the ground' (Ho. 2:18, RSV). For Jeremiah the certainty of such promises is based upon the reality of God's prior covenant with the forces of nature (Je. 33:25).

Once again we see how the Israelites interrelated social, moral and ecological orders. The relationships between God and humankind, within humankind, and between humankind and the non-human creation cannot be separated. A failure in any one of these areas implies a breakdown elsewhere.

iii. Redemption and the new creation: Probably the best known creation passages in the entire prophetic tradition occur in Isaiah 40 – 55. They pick up the positive strand in the prophetic tradition and use creation imagery as a way of expressing God's promise of redemption to the captives in Babylon.

Precisely because the passages are speaking about redemption rather than creation as such the critical consensus dismisses them as nothing more than an expression of redemption.[1] However, it is surely significant that in addressing the captives, Yahweh's promise of redemption is *underwritten* with creation imagery. The less certain is guaranteed by the more certain. The very use of such imagery implies an existing faith in a God who created *and sustains* the natural world. Without such a faith, Isaiah's promises of redemption would be incomprehensible.

3. New Testament perspectives

a. Nature in Jesus' teaching

There is no direct teaching about the natural world in the gospel accounts of Jesus' ministry. However, nature imagery does play an interesting part in his teaching about God's care for human beings. Typically it takes the form of an argument from the greater to the lesser (a favourite form of Jewish argumentation): from a more incredible (but mutually

[1] *E.g.* Reumann, 1973, p. 78.

accepted) proposition to the less incredible (but disputed) proposition.

For example, the assertion that God cares for something as insignificant as a sparrow becomes the basis for reassuring us that God cares for us (Lk. 12:6–7). The point is that God cares for individual human beings not that he cares for sparrows. However, the argument only works if Jesus' audience accepts the premise that God cares for individual sparrows. In other words, there is implicit in Jesus' teaching about God's fatherly care for human beings an affirmation of his fatherly care for even the least significant of creatures.

Another element in Jesus' teaching which has been picked up by some Christian traditions and developed with reference to the natural world, is his saying about the Holy Spirit in John 6:63: 'The Spirit gives life.' That phrase has been enshrined in the creeds as a central truth about the Spirit: he is 'the Lord, the Life-giver'. And that truth extends beyond a reference to the Spirit's role in sanctification.

b. Nature in Pauline Christianity

In spite of a bad press on other issues, recent attempts to develop a biblically based theology of nature have looked particularly to Paul and the Pauline tradition for inspiration. Two passages stand out as particularly important for a biblical doctrine of nature.

i. Romans 8:18–25: Paul makes these very significant comments about creation in the context of an exposition of what it means to live by faith. Specifically, in Romans 8 he is dealing with the new law of the Holy Spirit and the Spirit's gift of hope which points us towards our eschatological inheritance.

Paul's use of 'creation' in this context may be interpreted in many ways. It could refer to the entire created order: angelic, human and non-human. Alternatively, it could be used in a more restricted sense to refer to any one or any combination of these sub-orders. Interpretations which emphasize the human dimension of creation are widely accepted by commentators. However, they are rendered unlikely by the involuntary nature of the bondage to which creation is subjected (verse 20). It seems more satisfactory to conclude that Paul had in mind primarily the sub-human created order.

This interpretation leads to the bizarre image of a suffering nature: a natural order eagerly awaiting an *eschaton* which will, amongst other things, mark an end to its bondage. However, the notion of nature being subject to futility makes sense if we recall the Hebrew context of Paul's thought. The word he uses for futility is the one used by the Greek Old Testament for 'vanity' (*e.g.* Ec. 1:2). Here, it appears to be synonymous with 'bondage to decay' (verse 21). With its reference to 'groaning as in the pains of childbirth', the passage clearly points us to Genesis 3 for an explanation. Thus it seems likely that creation's inability to fulfil the purpose of its existence[1] is a direct result of the disorder envisaged in Genesis 3:17.

If so, the one who subjected it must be God. However, the responsibility for this state lies firmly with humankind: our place in the created order is such that our disobedience brings with it ecological consequences. Paul does not teach that nature is *in itself* fallen, rather its fulfilment is inextricably bound up with the destiny of humankind.[2] *Our* disobedience prevents the natural order from achieving *its* goal: creation 'is cheated of its true fulfilment so long as man, the chief actor in the drama of God's praise, fails to contribute his rational part'.[3]

In spite of this assessment, Paul emphasizes that hope is not excluded from creation. On the contrary, it was subjected 'in hope'. The present suffering is to be seen as birth pangs which ultimately will give way to joy and fulfilment. Paul sees Christ's redemptive activity as effecting not just the reconciliation of humanity with God but, through that, also the consummation of the entire created order. The non-human part of creation is not merely a dispensable backdrop to the human drama of salvation history, but is itself able to share in the 'glorious freedom' which Paul envisages for the covenant community. What we have here is a Christological and pneumatological (and, hence trinitarian) transformation of the Old Testament concept of human dominion.

ii. Colossians 1:15–20: This hymn of praise begins by claiming that Jesus Christ 'is the image of the invisible God,

[1]Cranfield, 1975, pp. 413f. [2]Westcott, 1890, p. 135.
[3]Cranfield, 1974, p. 227.

the firstborn over all creation' (verse 15). Both titles offer us perspectives on the relationship between creation and redemption.

The title 'firstborn' should not be interpreted along Hellenistic lines as meaning the first of creatures. On the contrary, it is a characteristically Jewish expression of pre-existence. As 'firstborn', all things were created in, through and for Jesus Christ. He is the agent of God's creative activity, the frame of reference for creation, the divine context of the created order and its eschatological end. These assertions are summarized in the statement that 'in him all things hold together' (verse 17). He is the sole basis of unity and purpose in the cosmos. In making these assertions, the hymn has identified Jesus Christ with divine wisdom: the personal basis of unity which allowed the Hebrews to discern a real correspondence between the moral and natural orders (*e.g.* Wisdom 9:4, 9; Pr. 8:22; Sirach 1:4; 24:9).

The hymn's identification of Jesus Christ as the image of God is a Christological reinterpretation of the Old Testament concept of humankind as the image of God. Thus the restoration of the image of God in humankind becomes part of the Christian vocation: we are called to be conformed to Christ, the paradigmatic image of God. At the same time the close connection made in the Old Testament between the divine image and humankind's dominion over the material creation means that the latter concept must undergo a similar transformation.

The hymn concludes with a reference to the cosmic significance of Christ's sacrifice (verses 19–20): his role in creation makes it appropriate to see him as reconciling to himself all things and not merely the community of believers or even the entire alienated human race. In making this assertion it maintains the link between redemption and creation (or new creation) made in the Old Testament (particularly through the notion of covenant and the use of creation imagery by the prophets).

c. *Nature in Johannine Christianity*

Interestingly, the Johannine tradition has fared much worse than the Pauline in recent studies of the biblical theology of nature. For example, Paul Santmire finds John's Gospel to be predominantly anti-ecological in tone, concluding that 'It is almost as if the dimensions of human history and the universal world of nature did not enter John's mind, except in terms of the negative connotations associated with his image of the "world".'[1]

However, this is hardly a fair summary of the Johannine attitude to nature. We have already noted that John's Gospel has bequeathed to Christianity a most profound insight into the role of the Holy Spirit as the Giver of Life. Significantly Santmire ignores the Prologue of John's Gospel in his discussion. In those verses we find the same identification of Christ with the creative divine wisdom that we saw so clearly in Colossians.

Arguably the main point at which the New Testament supplements Old Testament teaching on creation and nature is in its development of a Christological dimension to the doctrine. Contrary to the impression given by Santmire, the best known such passage is none other than the Prologue of John. There we are told that, 'Through him all things were made; without him nothing was made that has been made. In him was life . . .' (Jn. 1:3–4a).

Thus Christ, the agent of redemption, is also the agent of creation (maintaining the Old Testament link between creation and redemption). More important for present purposes is the assertion that 'in him was life'. Taken in conjunction with the Old Testament teaching that God is the continuing source of the life of all creatures, this implies not only the deity of Christ but his continuing involvement in the creative activity of God.

Furthermore, it stresses the sheer physicality of the incarnation (Jn. 1:14) in a way that contradicts the spiritualizing tendencies perceived by Santmire. The same theme appears still more forcefully in the First Letter of John.

As if that were not enough, Revelation makes it quite clear that the Johannine tradition did maintain an essentially positive attitude to the natural world. Chapter 4 presents a remarkable vision of the entire created order praising God. Is that order to be dissolved in the impending apocalypse? John's response is an unequivocal 'No!' The conclusion of

[1]Santmire, 1985, p. 213.

this series of visions is of the created order, not dissolved but transformed: 'a new heaven and a new earth' (Rev. 21:1). Nowhere is it suggested that the biophysical universe will cease to be. On the contrary, it too will share in the eschatological fulfilment prefigured by God's redemptive activity in relation to humankind. The concluding chapters of Revelation are nothing less than a word picture of the hope for creation expressed by Paul (Rom. 8:21).

4. Conclusions

The tendency to treat the non-human creation as a temporary expedient or resource finds no basis in the biblical texts we have examined. There are some biblical passages which suggest a divine transformation of the world (*e.g.* Is. 65:17–25 and Rev. 21 – 22), but nowhere is it suggested that the biophysical universe will cease to be. On the contrary, it is an integral part of the New Testament's eschatological vision.

This is further supported by the Old Testament's insistence on the goodness of the non-human creation (Gn. 1); God's fatherly care for even those aspects of nature which threaten humankind (Ps. 104); and its understanding of the non-human creation as the abiding context for divine–human encounter.

However, as I have already suggested, it is not enough to reply to the criticisms of the environmentalists by showing that the biblical traditions do not themselves advocate an exploitative approach. We must go on to look at ways in which that insight may cause us to revise our theology and our ethics.

CHAPTER SIX

In the beginning

1. Refreshing our view of God

In chapter 4 I outlined Gordon Kaufman's fear that greater theological attention to nature may lead to radical revision of our concept of God. As we begin the process of outlining a theology of creation capable of enabling us to respond constructively to the environmental crisis, I want to explore that suggestion a bit further.

a. Historical indicators

Environmentalist critiques of Christian theology tend to focus exclusively on western Christianity. It is a striking fact of history that the Christian east, equipped with similar intellectual, material, political and spiritual resources, did not give rise to an exploitative technology in the same way as its partner in Christendom. Was this merely an accident of history? Or can the cause be traced to significant philosophical and theological differences between west and east?

It is widely assumed that the Greeks and Romans had very different attitudes to technology. Greek culture is presented as more speculative, less interested in this world (which was regarded as nothing more than an imperfect reflection of the perfect world of ideas). The Romans, by contrast, are regarded as more practical: Roman ruins, still impressive two millennia later, bear eloquent witness to their practicality. Might the more recent western development of science and technology be related to that earlier divergence rather than the influence of Christian theology?

Such an explanation is tempting but is not borne out by closer investigation. It ignores the fact that by late Roman times Greek and Roman cultures had become inextricably joined to produce a single Hellenistic culture throughout the Mediterranean basin. Although the Empire eventually split into Latin and Greek speaking regions, this cannot be read as a simple reversion to earlier cultural divisions. In any case, transcending this political and linguistic division was a new common faith – Christianity. Only much later did it too split into eastern and western forms.

Lynn White argues that western Christianity was peculiarly adapted to encourage the growth of exploitative attitudes towards the natural world. However, in the east, a different understanding of the spiritual life hindered this adaptation: 'The Greek saint contemplates; the Western saint acts. The implications of Christianity would emerge more easily in the Western atmosphere.'[1] White has simply taken the view I have just criticized and transposed it into theological terms. The resultant sweeping generalization is easily contradicted. For example, Basil of Caesarea, one of the most influential of the Greek Fathers, has gone down in history as the founder of the western world's first hospital. He was also untiring in ministering to the needy (*e.g.* in famine relief work).[2] Conversely, it is also true that contemplation was as much a part of western spirituality as of eastern spirituality.[3]

However, there was a fundamental theological difference between the western and eastern churches; a disagreement about the nature of the Holy Trinity which ultimately led to the Great Schism between Roman Catholicism and Eastern Orthodoxy. The starting point for eastern trinitarianism was

[1]L. White, 1967, p. 1206. [2]Kaiser, 1991, pp. 41–44.

[3]It was certainly important to Augustine and the influence of his writings may be detected throughout the history of western spirituality. See *SS*, pp. 136–138.

the New Testament witness to three divine agents: Father, Son and Holy Spirit. All their efforts were devoted to showing that this could be reconciled with the Old Testament's insistence on the unity of God. In the west, however, Augustine opted for a different starting point. He accepted the Old Testament's witness to divine unity and asked how the one God could also be three. Ideally, of course, both approaches should have come to the same conclusion. In reality they reflect different assessments about what is most important about God. For Augustine and his western followers, divine unity was the fundamental datum. For the east, it was the diversity of divine action in creation and history which was fundamental.

Is there a corresponding divergence in attitudes to the material world?

It is very difficult to give a clear answer to this question because positive and negative statements about the material world can be found in both eastern and western theologies. However, examination of medieval stories about the relations between Christian saints and the non-human creation do seem to point in this direction. Helen Waddell has collected a large number of these stories in her charming book *Beasts and Saints*. The accounts of encounters between eastern saints and wild animals certainly suggest that a high degree of intimacy between human and non-human was widely regarded as characteristic of saints.

But was this not also true of western saints? A striking feature of Waddell's book is that, while her sources were Latin texts preserved by the western church, the western saints cited come exclusively from the Celtic tradition. A more recent book, charting the history of religious attitudes to nature, also suggests that such saints were drawn mostly from the Orthodox, Celtic and Franciscan traditions.[1]

In spite of its geographical location, the Celtic Church maintained its own distinctive approach to Christianity, largely independent of Roman Catholicism. Contrary to some recent suggestions, this approach was quite orthodox.[2] In

[1]Regenstein, 1991, pp. 58–69.

[2]Celtic spirituality has fallen under a shadow because of New Age attempts to explain its positive view of creation as the result of pagan Celtic influences. However, the orthodoxy of Celtic Christianity is clearly demonstrated by *SS*, pp. 216–225.

theology, spirituality and liturgical practice it retained significant links with the eastern churches. During a period when knowledge of Greek was rare in the western church, it was still taught in Ireland. In fact, it was an Irish-trained theologian, John Scotus Eriugena, who was responsible for bringing many of the major works of eastern theology to the attention of western theologians in the ninth century.[1] Like Eastern Orthodoxy, Celtic Christianity managed to retain a strong emphasis on trinitarianism. At the same time it viewed the material world positively as God's good creation.

What of the Franciscan tradition? Perhaps because he was not a theologian, St Francis himself was able to take seriously the trinitarian nature of God as indicated in the New Testament. Although in many ways his practice of Christianity was in keeping with medieval Roman Catholicism, he put a degree of emphasis on the Trinity which was unusual for his time. And, of course, he is best known for his insistence on the goodness of God's material creation. However, this combination did not last long. In order to secure the orthodoxy of the Franciscan order, its first great theologian, St Bonaventure, adopted a thoroughly Augustinian approach. For Bonaventure nature was like a ladder by which we ascend to God – but when we have reached God we no longer need the ladder.

The history of Christian attitudes to the natural world does seem to suggest that there is some degree of correlation between a positive view of creation and a faith in which trinitarianism plays an important part.

b. *Theological considerations*

Many theologians now consider the doctrine of the Trinity to have been crucial in shaping the development of other Christian doctrines. Its influence can be traced in the history of the doctrines of Christ, of salvation and of the church. This may seem surprising – after all, in the west, the doctrine of the Trinity is often presented as a highly abstract piece of theological speculation with little relevance to the daily reality of the Christian life. Two general arguments can be put forward to show why this is a mistake.

[1] *NDT*, p. 227.

i. The distinctiveness of Christianity: The doctrine of the Trinity is the distinguishing feature of Christian theology. This is because the form and content of theology are critically dependent on who God is and has revealed himself to be.

A theology which claims to be Christian necessarily refers its readers to the God who has revealed himself as a human person (Jesus Christ) at a specific time and place within the history of the universe. Indeed, it has been said of the Incarnation that, 'by thinking through the meaning of this event in terms of the Trinity one finds in embryo the key to the solution of God's relation to the world.'[1] If so, the only adequate basis for a Christian understanding of the world is the doctrine of the Trinity.

However, many classical western Christian doctrines of creation and providence have, effectively, ignored trinitarian thought. Instead they have tended to rely on a general philosophical monotheism rather than the Christian revelation of God as triune. The result has been a view of creation virtually indistinguishable from those of the other major monotheistic religions.[2]

The effect of this has been to turn creation and providence into apparently neutral ground. Because Christian, Jewish and Muslim views of providence appear to be identical, the doctrine comes to be regarded as public knowledge supposedly accessible to all men of good will and sound reason. As a result, it provides a justification for doing natural theology. But, at the same time, it creates room within theology for non-Christian concepts of God and natural analogies for the relationship between God and his creation. A distinctively Christian approach to providence would rule out both organismic and mechanistic analogies for the world. Their recurrence within Christian theology is suggestive of failure at this point.

ii. Providence and the Trinity: A theology of nature will be particularly concerned about God's continuing care for the non-human aspects of his creation. Thus it will be

[1]O'Donnell, 1983, p. 198.

[2]Typical is a recent study of providence whose results are claimed to be equally acceptable to those 'who hold to an orthodox variation of Christianity or Judaism or Islam' (Langford, 1981, p. 155).

continuous with a doctrine of providence. But providence lends itself to a trinitarian treatment.

Why is this? Providence is concerned with the maintenance of creatures in and through time and their being brought to an eschatological fulfilment. It has to do with divine action in creation history. Thus an adequate account of the doctrine of providence is bound up with an adequate Christian understanding of time.

This brings us back to the doctrine of the Trinity because, as I noted above, God has revealed himself as a person with a history embedded in the history of the human race and the cosmos as a whole. In other words, God has permitted himself to be identified in temporal terms: he is the one who raised Jesus from the dead.[1]

By contrast, the classical philosophical understanding of God is a timelessly eternal being. That view leads to insuperable difficulties for understanding the relationship between God and the world. How can a timeless God be related to a temporal creation?

The timelessness of God is often defended by the counter-question, 'If we say that the life of God is temporal do we not subject God to something which is not God?'

No we do not! The Christian doctrine of the Trinity speaks of a divine life which *defines* created temporality. Call the life of God eternal if you like. But it is a rich dynamic eternity. It is the reality: our experience of time is but its shadow.

c. *Interim conclusions*

Taken together, the historical indicators and the theological arguments point to the doctrine of the Trinity as the place where any revision of our understanding of God should concentrate its efforts. Western Christianity, in adhering to the ancient creeds of the church, has always paid lip-service to this doctrine. However, in practical terms, it has consistently neglected trinitarian theology.[2] Hence the apparent irrelevance of the doctrine to so many western Christians.

A re-examination of the doctrine of the Trinity is beyond the scope of this book. However, all that follows is built upon such a re-examination. I take for granted that God is best

[1]Jenson, 1982b, p. 21. [2]*E.g.* Rahner, 1970, p. 10.

understood as a Trinity of divine agents each with a distinctive role in the activity of creation. But, although there are three divine agents, creation is one work (just as there are three Persons but one God). An adequate doctrine of creation and providence will reflect this trinitarian structure. A similar structure is to be seen in orthodox soteriology where each of the three Persons has his own distinctive role in salvation but those roles are not separable.

Finally, a word of warning. In a recent book on the Holy Spirit, Tom Smail comments,

> A good map will not by itself get you where you should be, but it will point you in the right direction. A balanced trinitarianism will not by itself unite our life with God's life although it will help to draw our attention to what God is offering and what we have been missing till now.[1]

By the same token, a trinitarian doctrine of creation will not by itself overcome negative attitudes to God's good creation. It is my hope that it may draw attention to a more biblical assessment of creation. And that as we learn to live in the presence of the triune God we will also learn to treat his creation with greater respect.

With that in mind, let us consider what an explicitly trinitarian doctrine of creation might look like. In the rest of this chapter I shall concentrate on God's primordial creative activity (*creatio ex nihilo*). The next chapter will focus on his continuing role in creation and the future of creation.

2. Biblical characteristics of creation

Our re-examination of the biblical traditions concerning nature revealed two major characteristics of God's creative activity: God created from *nothing* and did so by means of a *word*.

[1]Smail, 1988, p. 136.

a. From 'nothing'?

On its own the first characteristic is ambiguous. Does it express the conviction that God is the exclusive cause of created being? Or does it speak of a 'nothingness', a primordial chaos from which God manufactured creation?

The latter interpretation immediately suggests that 'nothingness' is co-eternal with God. Thus his creative activity may be determined to some extent by the character of that chaos. Clearly this view compromises belief in God's sovereignty. Nevertheless, belief in an eternal void or chaos has emerged from time to time in western theology.

Most recently a version of this doctrine has appeared in the work of the German theologian Jürgen Moltmann. In arriving at this position he has drawn upon insights from the cosmological speculation of Jewish Cabbalism. Admittedly he does not regard the primordial chaos as co-eternal with God. On the contrary, it is created by God. It is a preparatory work brought about by 'a withdrawal by God into himself'.[1] The void is the created space within which creation occurs.

However, while avoiding any compromise of divine sovereignty, Moltmann's suggestion raises other difficulties. It makes creation the corollary of a primordial divine act of self-negation. This divine creativity is to be understood in terms of negation, emptying, humiliation. This is entirely in keeping with his presentation of Christ's redemptive work and recalls the Lutheran tendency to understand love as self-hatred. However, it patently does not cohere with the entirely positive note struck by the biblical accounts of creation.

b. Creation by word

The second characteristic of creation, its status as a divine speech-act, effectively eliminates the ambiguity of the first. In the beginning, God spoke. Creation is a positive act of divine expression: it is rooted entirely in God. Creation owes nothing to any alien 'nothingness' standing in opposition to God. Furthermore, it is positively rooted in God: creation does not flow from some divine act of self-negation.

Some writers have suggested that creation by word is a kind of magical operation. For example, they point to

[1]Moltmann, 1985, p. 86.

parallels in Egyptian creation myths. Similarly, Jewish and Christian Cabbalists built up elaborate magical systems on the assumption that God created by uttering permutations of the divine name (or of the Hebrew alphabet). However, such an interpretation could be valid only if God created from a co-eternal chaos. In this case, the divine speech might be thought to evoke order from the chaos. If we adopt the traditional understanding of creation from nothing, there can be nothing magical about it.

But why present creation as a speech-act if there is nothing magical about it? This way of describing creation has both positive and negative implications for our attempts to construct a theology of creation.

Negatively, creation as a divine speech-act rules out a variety of speculative theories about the world's origins. In particular, it contradicts the ever popular metaphors of diffusion and overflow. These pantheistic metaphors render creation impersonal – it becomes an uncontrolled and arbitrary event. If creation is the impersonal overflow of divine substance, then God cannot be in control of himself let alone be sovereign over that overflow. Thus the world is essentially alienated deity and redemption must be reinterpreted as the quest for victory over this alienation (*i.e.*, over creatureliness).

Positively, it underlines Hebrew and Christian faith in the sovereignty of God. It also rules out any doctrine of creation which would present it primarily in terms of divine self-fulfilment. Furthermore, a speech-act is essentially intelligible. Thus creation should not be thought of as in any way capricious. Finally, it implies that creation is divine expression: thus any Christian doctrine of creation entails the prior development of an appropriate understanding of God.

3. Creation as a trinitarian act

It follows from the preceding sections that a distinctively Christian doctrine of creation may not be developed independently of a doctrine of the Trinity. If creation is a personal, sovereign and rational act of the God who has revealed himself in Christ Jesus, it is an act of the triune God.

Unfortunately the Augustinian way of understanding the

Trinity effectively isolated the Trinity from creation. Augustine put so much stress on the inseparability of the external acts of the divine Persons that they became indistinguishable. One notorious result of this was the difficulty he had in explaining why it was the Son rather than the Father or the Spirit who became incarnate.

In order to produce a trinitarian account of creation we must be able to distinguish the roles of the Persons. Although he never explicitly criticized Augustine's theology, John Calvin was prepared to make such distinctions. In his account of the Trinity he stresses the role of the Father as 'the beginning of activity, and the fountain and wellspring of all things'. Similarly the Son and the Spirit are given distinctive roles: 'to the Son, wisdom, counsel, and the ordered disposition of all things; but to the Spirit is assigned the power and efficacy of that activity'.[1]

In making these distinctions Calvin has adopted an approach akin to that of the Cappadocian Fathers who formulated the Nicene Creed. Like them he had a dynamic understanding of the Trinity. This is underlined by his tendency to use verbs rather than nouns when speaking of the being of God. God has revealed his incomprehensible essence in his activity. Thus the unity of God is not to be sought in some hypothetical timeless static being, but in the inexhaustible life of the divine Persons in relationship with one another: a life which is revealed by the very diversity of God's activity of creation, redemption and consummation.

Applying such a trinitarianism to creation we may say that the Father creates, the Son creates and the Spirit creates. This does not mean merely that the one God creates in a way that may be understood under three purely symbolic headings. Rather, there are three personal agents of the one act of creation. On the other hand, the inseparability of the three Persons precludes any understanding of creation which would ascribe it exclusively to one of the Persons. Thus, one of the Cappadocian Fathers could say that,

> We do not learn that the Father does something on

[1]Calvin, *Inst.*, 1.13.18.

> his own, in which the Son does not co-operate. Or again, that the Son acts on his own without the Spirit. Rather does every operation which extends from God to creation and is designated according to our differing conceptions of it have its origin in the Father, proceed through the Son, and reach its completion by the Holy Spirit.[1]

In summary, we may say that the work of creation is a single divine act which is the joint work of three agents whose roles in the one work are distinguished in a manner analogous to and deriving from the inner-trinitarian distinctions of the Persons.

a. Triune activity or tritheism?

This concept of triune activity raises a serious difficulty in the western mind. In what sense can one speak of three agents for a single act? This problem has been effectively suppressed by the monistic tendency of Augustinian doctrines of the Trinity. However, it is implicit in criticisms which represent the above approach as inherently tritheistic. Our understanding of agency and individuality is such that we tend to see a multiplicity of agents as a multiplicity of individuals: three divine agents implies three gods.

A similar difficulty occurs within the doctrine of providence. How can both God and a human individual be held responsible for a specific act without a profound violation of human freedom?

The latter problem (of double agency) is closely connected with the modern understanding of freedom. One effect of the change in the historical consciousness of western society which accompanied the Enlightenment was a transformation in the concept of freedom.[2] Traditionally Christian theology understood human freedom in terms of vocation: freedom lay in responding to God's will for you. In western society this has given way to an understanding of freedom as autonomy. Instead of divine agency being seen as enabling creaturely agency, they are regarded as competing. Kathryn Tanner suggests that when theology attempts to maintain this new

[1]Gregory of Nyssa, *Abl.*, pp. 261f. [2]Gilkey, 1976, p. 193.

concept of freedom one of two things can happen. It may deny divine sovereignty, making creation autonomous of the creator (deism). Alternatively, it may attempt to maintain divine sovereignty by making the creature a moment in the life of God (pantheism).[1]

Only by rejecting the modern understanding of human freedom can this aspect of the doctrine of providence be seen to be coherent. Similarly, the coherence of the notion of triune activity depends on a rejection of any concept of personhood built upon such a view of freedom.

b. The creative speech-act as trinitarian

Theologians have attempted to assign aspects of the work of creation to the divine Persons in a variety of ways. One modern example is that of the Lutheran theologian, Robert Jenson:

> Insofar as 'the world is created' is equivalent to 'the world has been commanded (to be),' creation is the work of the Father. Insofar as 'the world is created' is equivalent to 'the world now is (by God's command),' creation is the work of the Son. Insofar as 'the world is created' is equivalent to 'the world is (commanded now) to be for God's purpose,' creation is the work of the Spirit. But these are one work; that they happen is one event.[2]

Following Reformed tradition, he has analysed the act of creation into the activities of origination, sustenance and consummation which he has then appropriated to Father, Son and Holy Spirit respectively. Similar schemes of appropriation may be found in Eastern Orthodoxy. For example,

> The work of creation is common to the whole Trinity, but each of the three persons is the cause of created being in a way which is different though in each case united to the others. ... 'In the creation, ... consider first the primordial cause ... of all that has been made – this is the Father; then the

[1]Tanner, 1988, pp. 164f. [2]Jenson, 1982a, p. 41.

> operating cause . . . which is the Son; and the perfecting cause . . . the Holy Spirit.'[1]

In both cases the historical character of God's creative activity is brought out by referring the different aspects of that activity to the three 'dimensions' of created time. Thus, origination refers to the absolute past of created being; sustenance refers to the actual course of created history; and consummation refers to the absolute future of creation.

In chapter 5 I suggested that the creative speech-act may be interpreted as holding out a divine promise to creation: it offers creation the gift of a future with God. Now, following the above examples, if we attempt to relate the roles of the Persons of the Trinity to this promise we come to the following formulation.

The Father is the source of the promise, the one who makes the primordial commitment to the creature, the Creator of heaven and earth. The Son is the mediator of the promise, the one who, before time and in time, enables the promise to be fulfilled, the one through whom all things were created. The Holy Spirit is the fulfilment of the promise, the one for whom the Son makes straight a path, the Lord and giver of life.

4. The promise of the Father

The divine *fiat*, the primordial expression of the promise, constitutes the background for any theological discussion of created being, human as well as non-human.

A promise is a commitment of oneself to a course of action intended to achieve some end on behalf of another or others. Casting creation in these terms, it is first and foremost God's gracious giving of himself to his creation. Far from being the self-negation envisaged by Moltmann, it is a divine act of self commitment.[2] Thus it involves God's acceptance of responsibility for his creation and this, in turn, provides a basis for a doctrine of God's providential care for his creation.

[1] Lossky, 1957, p. 100, citing Basil of Caesarea. [2] Thunberg, 1965, p. 86.

It implies that the object of creation be so structured that God may appropriately commit himself to it. Again, interpreting the word of creation as promise rather than command suggests that these structures are better thought of as open-ended: an incomplete, contingent order which offers a framework for cosmic evolution. Indeed, since there is no preceding structure to be overcome, it suggests an entirely contentless initial state: the mere possibility of subsequent finite ordering.

The Father's promise is a divine commitment to this void: a commitment to the maintenance and fulfilment of its structures, and to the evocation of ever-more complex substructures within it. This personal giving of himself to creation entails a commitment to guide the evolution of its structures so as to enable its appropriate response.

5. Implications for the Kingdom of Nature

What are the implications of this view of creation for our understanding of the non-human?

If creation is a divine promise, then to be is to be one to which or to whom God has promised himself. This implies that every creature is an object of divine love. For this reason, and contrary to the intuitions of Augustinian Christianity, the non-human creation *is* worthy of our respect and interest.

If creaturely being entails divine self-commitment, it follows that to be is to be related to the triune God. The doctrines of the Trinity and of creation, taken together, point to the necessity of a metaphysics in which (personal) relationships are fundamental. Thus, creaturely being will be understood as rooted in relationships and processes rather than in things or individual events.

The personal relationships within the Trinity constitute the paradigm for all creaturely relationships. This is clear in the way in which God chooses to reveal himself to his creation. The person of Jesus Christ is the final point of contact between God and the world.[1] In the hypostatic union, Creator and creature become one and indivisible without any

[1]Meyendorff, 1983, p. 36.

loss of their distinctive natures, without any confusion. There is an absolute difference but no distance between Creator and created.

Such a metaphysics gives rise to two very important affirmations about creation both human and non-human. It guarantees the free reality of creatures by protecting the otherness of the creature. A personal relationship as the basis of creaturely being precludes the possibility of a pantheistic dissolution of God in creation or the creature in God. Closely related to this is the fact that it guarantees the freedom of the creature and the contingency of creation as a whole.[1] This implies that creation as a whole is radically historical: history is not just a function of human culture. Contingency also reminds us that the initial creation was an act of absolute novelty.[2] Creation is essentially dynamic.

[1]Zizioulas, 1985, p. 39; Thunberg, 1965, p. 69. [2]Young, 1976, p. 149.

CHAPTER SEVEN

The Kingdom of Nature

A theology of creation which restricts itself to the beginnings of things is entirely inadequate. God's creative activity cannot be confined to the act of origination. On the contrary, it embraces the entire history of the universe from its origin to its ultimate end. As Calvin points out,

> to make God a momentary Creator, who once for all finished his work, would be cold and barren, and we must differ from profane men especially in that we see the presence of the divine power shining as much in the continuing state of the universe as in its inception . . . For unless we pass on to his providence – however we may seem both to comprehend with the mind and to confess with the tongue – we do not yet properly grasp what it means to say: 'God is Creator.'[1]

[1]Calvin, *Inst.*, 1.16.1.

In this chapter I shall take his advice and pass on to an examination of providence. In recent centuries the doctrine of providence has often been effectively restricted to God's general dealings with humankind. However, properly understood, providence also embraces those aspects of creation which are most closely related to contemporary environmental concerns, namely, God's continuing care for what he has created and the end for which it was created.

1. Sustaining the Kingdom of Nature

a. Sustenance as trinitarian activity

An essential part of any doctrine of providence is some account of God's gracious preservation (maintenance or sustenance) of what he has created. Given the above account of creation, we may regard this aspect of God's creative activity as appropriately the work of the Son (while rejecting any suggestion that it might be exclusive to the second Person of the Trinity).

i. The meaning of sustenance: The doctrine of divine sustenance affirms that the God who has once acted to create a finite contingent order remains faithful to that order and the creatures within it. God maintains created being in and through time: sustenance is the continuation of creation. Negatively, God preserves creation against the threat of dissolution into non-existence. Positively, God nurtures creation towards a specific end: there is a dynamic, developmental (even, progressive) element within the doctrine.

This latter aspect is sometimes emphasized by use of the term 'continuous creation'. However, there are two very real dangers associated with such an emphasis.

The first danger is the temptation to drop the notion of original creation. Too strong an emphasis on God's present creative activity may cause his past creative activity to drop out of sight. But this has the effect of distorting our understanding of God: instead of the living God who is sovereign over past, present and future, we are left with a concept of God as exclusively present. This, in turn, forces a co-ordination between God and creation which leads inexorably back to pantheism.[1]

The other danger is that a concept of continuous creation may tempt us to reduce sustenance to continuous origination. Thus,

> the duration of a thing which has remained almost unchanged through years or centuries, or millions of years, is . . . not a static being which exists in itself, but a continuous series of successive acts of preservation, by which from moment to moment it is decided afresh that this thing shall retain this particular form.
>
> Thus all maintenance is a continuous re-creation.[2]

Implicit in this is a denial of creaturely persistence. Temporal succession is mere illusion: an artefact of the succession of acts of creation. By thus undermining the status of time in the created order, the doctrine of re-creation effectively denies the central content of the doctrine of preservation or sustenance. It also undermines the freedom of created being. Created activity is necessarily temporal. If temporality is an illusion and the reality is a series of divinely ordained static moments of creation, there can be no genuine activity on the part of the creature but only the illusion of activity. And without the reality of creaturely activity it is futile to speak of creaturely freedom.

In order to maintain the dynamic dimension of the doctrine while avoiding the dangers implicit in continuous creation, I use the term 'sustenance'.[3] It also avoids the negative connotations of preservation and conservation.[4] This organic metaphor maintains the dynamic nature of conservation without suggesting that the end in view is external to the object of sustenance. It speaks of the nourishing and bringing to maturity of creation. Finally, it reminds us that God's creative activity subsequent to the act of origination is a creation on the basis of and in organic

[1]Weber, 1981, pp. 504f. [2]Heim, 1935, p. 182.

[3]Berkouwer, 1952, pp. 50–82.

[4]Preservation suggests maintenance of the *status quo* or restoration of a former state. Conservation suggests maintenance with an end in view, but this is invariably anthropocentric (Passmore, 1980, p. 73).

continuity with what has already been created.[1]

ii. Sustenance is trinitarian: At first sight an exclusively Christocentric account of this doctrine would be in accord with the New Testament. After all, Paul says of the cosmic Christ, 'in him all things were created ... all things were created through him and for him. He is before all things, and in him all things hold together' (Col. 1:16–17, RSV).

However, he adds that 'in him all the fulness of God was pleased to dwell, and *through him* to reconcile to himself all things' (Col. 1:19–20a, RSV). This reminds us that sustenance, like any divine activity, is an activity of the whole Trinity. Calvin makes this explicit by ascribing the work of sustaining creation to both the Son and the Holy Spirit.[2]

In order to reflect the trinitarian nature of sustenance, I shall look first at the role of the Son and then examine how sustenance relates back to origination (appropriated to the Father) and forward to consummation (appropriated to the Holy Spirit).

b. The sustaining power of the Son

As I have already explained, I take sustenance to mean the maintenance of what has been originated by God with a view to its ultimate consummation. Thus, sustenance is the historical activity which draws creation from its original state to that final state which is God's ultimate purpose for it. In a sense it reconciles the original creation with the new heavens and new earth of the *eschaton.* It is appropriately regarded as an activity of the Son precisely because there is a sense in which it is analogous with his other reconciling activity. Hence the Prologue to John's Gospel can present the Son as the source of life in the broadest possible sense. Just as the Son through his incarnation, death, resurrection and sending of the Spirit brings spiritual life to humankind, so through his sustaining activity he gives life to all creation. As Calvin comments,

[1]Exodus is a biblical paradigm of this new creation. God does a new thing which was humanly speaking quite unpredictable, indeed impossible, and which gives rise to a wealth of new possibilities for creaturely being. Nevertheless it stands in organic continuity with the sweep of created history (Jenson, 1982b, p. 35).

[2]*E.g.* he refers to the sustaining activity of the Son in *Inst.*, 1.13.8 and *C.Jn.*, 1.4 and to that of the Spirit in *Inst.*, 1.13.14 and *Praed.*, 10.1.

'Were it not that his continued inspiration gives vigour to the world, every thing that *lives* would immediately decay, or be reduced to nothing.'[1]

Another way of looking at the sustaining activity of the Son is in relation to his status as the Word or Speech of God. The connection between words and reason was certainly not lost on the authors of the New Testament. Viewed in this way, Christ is the source of the rational order which we observe in the cosmos – an order without which there could be no life.

Christ is the one who shapes creaturely existence.[2] But this shaping cannot be understood apart from the original state which is its starting point, and the *eschaton* which is its goal. Thus Christ preserves what has been originated, maintaining it against the threat of dissolution into the original state of creation.[3] However, as has been suggested by my use of the term sustenance, there is a positive aspect to this creative work of Christ. His shaping of existence is no mere preservation of past structures. On the contrary, an essential dimension of sustenance is the evocation of new dimensions – new levels – of order and complexity. Nor is this the mere evocation of novelty for novelty's sake – there is a definite end in view.

c. Origination and sustenance

Sustenance is the maintenance or continuation of original creation. Therefore it must be understood in the light of that act of origination.

The original act of creation was an act of loving communication based upon a divine decision: 'To be is to be addressed' by the Father.[4] The doctrine of divine sustenance teaches that this address did not occur once and for all. It rules out the deistic notion of creaturely persistence as merely the immanent unfolding of a past divine act. On the contrary, the Father continues to address his creation.

The content of that address is the history of Jesus. The Son

[1]Calvin, *C.Jn.*, 1.4. [2]Hardy & Ford, 1984, p. 119.

[3]The references to formlessness and void in Gn. 1:2 strongly suggest a primordial state of chaos. In terms of modern physics this would be a state of universal thermal equilibrium similar to the final state envisaged by many secular scientific visions of the far future.

[4]Jenson, 1973, p. 134.

is the Word of God addressed to all creatures and not merely humanity. Thus it is, through Jesus the Son, that 'all things hold together'. This implies a striking affirmation of the biophysical universe. God addresses his creatures by entering into creation.[1] Creation itself and not some transcendent realm of ideas is the divinely appointed location for the encounter between God and the creature.

Also implicit in this view of sustenance is a denial of contemporary secular eschatologies based on the indefinite extrapolation of our present understanding of the physical universe. Current cosmological models suggest that, left to itself, the universe would eventually degenerate to a state of universal thermal equilibrium. In this state, the physical universe would have achieved maximum entropy (a measure of disorder) and stability. Life could not exist in such a universe. Matter/energy would have been reduced to its simplest building blocks. It would have returned to the 'waste and void' of Genesis 1:2.

The doctrine of divine sustenance denies that this is the final state of the universe. Our God is a God of order. Thus, faith in sustenance must reject the universal applicability of the second law of thermodynamics, a belief which was virtually the central dogma of classical physics.[2] This negative aspect of divine sustenance might be summarized by saying that, through Christ, creation is enabled to resist entropy and, hence, disorder.

d. *Sustenance and fulfilment*

Many of the cosmological models which most clearly portray the end of the universe as a state of universal thermal equilibrium are also deterministic.[3] This suggests that the doctrine of divine sustenance affirms genuine creaturely freedom and

[1]Jüngel, 1976, pp. 2f.; Steck, 1980, p. 267.

[2]*E.g.* the great Quaker astrophysicist, Sir Arthur Eddington, once commented that 'the Second Law of Thermodynamics holds, I think, the supreme position among the laws of Nature. ... if your theory is found to be against the Second Law of Thermodynamics I can give you no hope; there is nothing for it but to collapse in deepest humiliation' (cited by Barrow & Tipler, 1986, p. 658).

[3]Most closed cosmological models (those which predict that ultimately the big bang will be succeeded by a big crunch) satisfy a topological condition known as Strong Cosmic Censorship; a condition which approximates to Laplacean determinism.

implies divine resistance to any tendency for the universe to degenerate into a deterministic state. It also justifies Pannenberg's insistence that Christ's work in relation to creation should be seen as reconciliation rather than determination.[1] Christ shapes creaturely existence – but not as an archetype. He is not a pre-existent pattern to which creation must conform. Thus, creation is free to be a unique contingent and historical reality.

What of the eschatological aspect? How do the Son and the Holy Spirit co-operate in the activity of sustaining created being?

Without this aspect, sustenance would degenerate into preservation; the history of creation would become a mere maintenance of the *status quo* laid down in the act of origination. It is the eschatological call of the Holy Spirit that distinguishes creation from the static harmony of the Hellenistic cosmos. He is the perfecting cause of creation; the agent of its consummation.

One aspect of sustenance is the movement towards this consummation. The pneumatological aspect is to be found in the liberation of the creature from bondage to history; from the persistence of the past. 'To be, says the gospel, is not to persist; it is rather to be surprised, to be called out of what I have and might persist in, to what I do not have.'[2] To the extent that sustenance is the maintenance of a history that is progressing in this way, it is an activity of the Holy Spirit. It follows that the Spirit's activity of consummation is not merely trans-historical. On the contrary, moments of partial consummation (steps towards the *eschaton*) are to be found in creation history.

Looked at in this light, the incarnation is a prefiguring of the *telos*, the End, of creation. The hypostatic union of God and creature in Jesus of Nazareth both prefigures and evokes an eschatological 'hypostatic' union between the triune God and creation.[3]

God is thus the ground of novelty: continually evoking new

[1] Pannenberg, 1968, p. 395.

[2] Jenson, 1973, p. 138. The original context of this quotation was a Christian anthropology. Here it is extended to cover the novelty which is observed to be a real part of creation history.

[3] Meyendorff, 1983, p. 36.

structures in a manner which 'diverges' towards the *eschaton*.[1] Ultimately such a God is not limited by the limitations of his creation at any historical epoch. On the contrary, the God who revealed himself in the histories of Israel and of Jesus, has revealed himself to be essentially one who is able to create new possibilities in every situation.

2. The end of the Kingdom

a. *The Holy Spirit and the fulfilment of creation*

We come now to the cosmic implications of Pentecost. The indwelling of the Holy Spirit in the church implies his indwelling in creation. But how are we to understand the role of the Holy Spirit in creation?

According to the Nicene Creed, the most fundamental title of the Holy Spirit, the role which determines all his other roles, is *zoopoioun*: the Giver of Life. For twentieth-century thought this title conveys an irreducible mystery, since life, in spite of the importance of the concept, has never been adequately defined.[2]

Although many Christians have understood the Spirit's role as life-giver in purely soteriological terms, the New Testament itself is not so restrictive. For example, Paul clearly relates life-giving spirit to the breath of life (1 Cor. 15:45). In so doing, he makes a clear connection between spirit as the new existence in humankind and the Hebrew (and Greek) conception of spirit as the universal source of life. While, in Genesis 1, the gift of life is presented as the adornment of the orders of creation. Both presentations point to the responsiveness of creation towards the creator. Thus the gift of life is intimately related to the *telos* (End) of creation.

The role of the Holy Spirit has been strongly affirmed within the Eastern Orthodox traditions (primarily as a way of affirming the deity of the Holy Spirit) and John Calvin clearly

[1]I might have used 'convergence' but this could suggest a determinate end-state towards which God is manipulating all things.

[2]Lovelock, 1988, pp. 16–18.

followed this lead in his own treatment of the deity of the Spirit:

> It is the Spirit who, everywhere diffused, sustains all things, causes them to grow, and quickens them in heaven and in earth. Because he is circumscribed by no limits, he is excepted from the category of creatures; but in transfusing into all things his energy, and breathing into them essence, life, and movement, he is indeed plainly divine.[1]

By contrast, more Augustinian theologies have tended to relegate the Spirit to the role of divine assistant in the sanctification of individual human beings.[2] As a corrective to this tendency, any contemporary doctrine of creation must explicitly discuss the role of the Holy Spirit.

The Holy Spirit, like the Father and the Son, is intimately involved in every aspect of God's creative activity. However, the trinitarian scheme presented above suggests that the aspect of creation most appropriate to the Spirit is the eschatological horizon: the consummation of creation.

But how are we to understand the consummation or fulfilment of the non-human creation? The key, I believe, lies in the Creed's insistence that the Holy Spirit is the one who gives life to creation: it is the fulfilment of his life-giving activity. This ought to rule out any suggestion that Christianity envisages a non-material, trans-historical *eschaton*: will the one who gives life to creation blot out all but a small portion of it at the last? It is, of course, true that just such a view has dominated much of the history of Christian theology. A purely spiritual *eschaton* is the corollary of an intellectualistic understanding of spirit. When spirit is equated with mind, life may be seen solely in terms of (conscious) mental processes and the non-rational becomes the non-living, as in Cartesian thought.

As we saw in chapter 4, the writings of Teilhard de Chardin offer us a vision of the eschatological bringing to life of

[1]Calvin, *Inst.*, 1.13.14.

[2]This tendency is part of a broader neglect of pneumatology engendered by an Augustinian doctrine of the Trinity. There are, of course, notable exceptions to this general trend, *e.g.* John Owen, Jonathan Edwards and Abraham Kuyper.

the cosmos. However, from the perspective of a doctrine of the non-human creation, his was a flawed vision. He made the Augustinian assumption that life and spirit are to be understood entirely in terms of human consciousness.

A very different understanding of consummation is forthcoming if we revert to a Hebrew view of life. In Hebrew thought, the chief characteristic of life is activity. Thus life becomes a far broader category than when it is understood in intellectualistic terms. For example, the activity of flowing water is sufficient to warrant the description 'living' (Gn. 26:19). The bringing to life of the cosmos is its transformation from passivity and inertia to activity. This is not to be understood in terms of a simple linear progression. Since its origin, the cosmos has harboured elements of both passivity and activity. The Holy Spirit is the ultimate (or final) source of all created activity and life (understood as that which tends towards the eschatological activity of the cosmos).

However, this is not a sufficient account of the Holy Spirit's life-giving activity. The Spirit does not evoke activity merely for its own sake. The eschatological goal of the non-human creation is not merely aimless autonomous activity. On the contrary, the life/activity evoked by the Holy Spirit will also be characterized by the Holy Spirit. The Holy Spirit is the one who makes possible and shapes our worship. By analogy, he is the one who enables creation as a whole to respond to God. 'The heavens declare the glory of God; the skies proclaim the work of his hands' (Ps. 19:1). But it is the Holy Spirit who orchestrates and conducts this cosmic symphony of worship.

There is also a clear connection between the doctrine of the Holy Spirit as the giver of life and the doctrine of the Son of God as the one who reconciles the cosmos to himself. We have already seen how the Christological dimension of creation may be developed in terms of resistance to entropy (*i.e.*, static equilibrium) and evocation of novelty (which implies ever-increasing complexity). The creative activity of the Holy Spirit may be seen in precisely parallel terms. Just as in traditional soteriology, the Son reconciles and the Spirit redeems. The work of the Holy Spirit is the necessary consequence of the Son's reconciliation of all things to himself. With the Son, the Spirit is the agent of novelty. To be more precise, as Jonathan Edwards suggested,[1] he is the beautifier of creation and the agent of its fulfilment.

b. The Sabbath of creation

On the face of it, the above comments stand in clear contradiction to that most fundamental biblical symbol of the *eschaton*: the Sabbath rest.

Jürgen Moltmann has done much to develop the doctrine of the Sabbath in the context of an ecological doctrine of creation. He presents the Sabbath as a time which has been sanctified so that it might symbolize the completion of creation. 'It is a completion through rest. Out of God's rest spring the blessing and sanctification of the seventh day.'[2] It symbolizes God's confrontation of his creation and its corollary, creation's co-existence with God. Furthermore, if the divine rest is to be taken seriously, the Sabbath of creation is also indicative of God's immanence in creation.[3] Thus the consummation of creation is to be understood as 'the completion given through the reposeful presence of the Creator in what he has created.'[4]

Moltmann claims that rest is the fulfilment of activity, being is the completion of doing. However, in the process, he has succeeded in presenting rest as opposed to activity. The general impression that one is left with is that rest fulfils activity by being its negation (just as, in much classical thought, eternity fulfils time by negating it).

i. The Sabbath and fulfilment: In order to avoid this impression it would perhaps be preferable to present rest as fulfilled activity rather than the fulfilment *of* activity.

Activity and rest are not direct opposites. The Sabbath rest is an active rest typified by the temple worship. Other biblical metaphors for the *eschaton* also bring out this emphasis on an active rest. Amongst these the most notable is perhaps the vision of the Kingdom as a place of feasting and enjoyment. The Sabbath rest is the active enjoyment of God and his blessings.

In other words, the rest which characterizes the *eschaton* is

[1]Edwards, 1971, pp. 108ff. [2]Moltmann, 1985, p. 278. [3]*Ibid.*, p. 280. [4]*Ibid.*, p. 287.

not passivity but the active rest in which all creation joins together in the praise of God. It is the unbounded fulfilment of the partial jubilation already audible in creation.

A possible physical metaphor would be that of sympathetic vibration and resonance. God has called creation into being; not an arbitrary chaos or a static cosmos but a world with the potential to respond to the divine call. Subsequently God has spoken his Word to creation with a view to evoking the appropriate response. The first stumbling responses are met with renewed divine address, encouraging a stronger response and so on *ad infinitum.* The *eschaton* corresponds to the to-us-incomprehensible state of completely unbounded divine address and creaturely response: an infinite spiral of blessing and praise.[1]

This is the vision behind the final stanza of the Philippian hymn (Phil. 2:9–11): and this again reminds us of the essential Christological dimension which is not lost even in the ultimate fulfilment of all things. If the Holy Spirit is the one who orchestrates and conducts this eschatological song of creation, the Son is its theme and the Father its original composer.

But the Sabbath rest is primarily a *divine* rest. The ultimate fulfilment of all things is, in a sense, also the divine self-fulfilment. This should not be taken as implying any defect in God which the act of creation seeks to overcome. Rather, it refers to the fulfilment of the divine promise. The eschatological Sabbath is a time when God is able to give himself fully to creation[2] and creation is able to respond fully. It represents the complete participation of creation in the triune life of God.[3]

Seen in this light the Spirit's eschatological bringing to life of the cosmos is, in a sense, nothing less than its deification. Eastern Orthodoxy has traditionally presented the work of the Spirit in humankind as *theiosis*: God graciously calls us to participate in the triune life.[4] It seems appropriate to extend this to the Spirit's work in relation to the non-human creation.

[1]This is a recurring theme of Hardy & Ford, 1984.

[2]With appropriate qualifications this may be symbolized as the divine embodiment in creation (*e.g.* Moltmann, 1985, pp. 13–17).

[3]Zizioulas, 1985, p. 50.

[4]We share in God's life rather than becoming gods in our own right.

ii. The present and the Sabbath: Much of twentieth-century experience would suggest that the present stands in direct contradiction of this vision of the future. However, the Christian vision of the future does not depend on history visibly tending towards the *eschaton* as a curve towards its asymptote. Eschatology does not imply a doctrine of progress.

It is more appropriate to regard certain moments in history as anticipations of the *eschaton*. The paradigm would be the history of Jesus.[1] However, there are such moments in the life of the church, of society and of every individual believer.

c. Implications for the non-human creation

The simplest, most obvious and yet most important implication of all this for the non-human creation is that it too will be an integral part of the eschatological spiral of blessing and praise. This conclusion contrasts sharply with traditional Christian views of the *eschaton* as purely spiritual and trans-historical. However, it is entirely consistent with the unashamedly materialistic eschatological imagery of the Bible.

We may also recall that the Spirit is the giver of life. All life is the gift of God. Every living creature receives its existence as a divine gift. As we shall see in the next chapter, this may be used to reinterpret the *dominium terrae*.

Can anything be said about the mode of giving? If it is seen in the light of the divine self-giving, we may rule out certain interventionist models. The gift of life is not merely extrinsic: it is not the superposition of spirit upon a dead mechanism. Dualism and interventionism remain intellectual possibilities but they are not encouraged by the Christian insistence that all life has the character of divine gift.

Neither is life to be dismissed as a mere by-product of material realities. This position is simply an inversion of the Cartesian view.

Finally, the Spirit's role as final cause or agent of eschatological transformation suggests that teleology ought to be rehabilitated as a way of speaking about created realities.

[1]Pannenberg, 1968, p. 392.

CHAPTER EIGHT

The guardians of creation: humankind and nature

1. Introduction

I suspect that some readers will be tempted to start here. This may be particularly true of those who are already convinced of the claims of the environment, or those who regard theology as too abstract to be of any relevance to every-day Christian living. Why wade through a long theological preamble?

Such a reaction is understandable. Until relatively recently western theology has shown little interest in the environment, much less the practicalities of caring for God's creation. Too often our life in this world had been regarded as a hiatus between conversion and some future, purely spiritual destiny (the beatific vision). The consequent dearth of theological attention to the natural world has left Christians without a firm theological base from which to answer the challenge of environmentalism.

At the same time, the lack of such a theological base has tended to obscure the essential link between theology and any *Christian* environmental ethic. Thus Christian environmentalists are tempted to respond in one of two ways.

Some Christian environmentalists explicitly base their environmental ethics on non-theological premises. While it is quite legitimate for a Christian to act upon such insights (provided they do not conflict with Christian belief), they cannot be urged upon other Christians. Thus environmentalism may be marginalized as a special interest shared by some Christians but not an integral part of their faith.

Alternatively, those with a high view of Scripture may attempt to read environmental principles straight out of the Bible. However, as we saw in chapter 5, it is notoriously difficult to avoid reading passionately held presuppositions *into* Scripture. Although it sounds biblical because it quotes Scripture, this option may, in practice, be indistinguishable from the previous one. Arguably it is less honest – hiding one's prejudices behind a smokescreen of Bible verses.

Either way, if the governing principles are drawn from non-Christian sources, such an environmental ethic may actually threaten Christian theology. The danger is similar to that of natural theology. Following Lord Gifford,[1] Karl Barth defined natural theology as

> a science of God, of the relations in which the world stands to Him and of the human ethics and morality resulting from the knowledge of Him. This science is to be constructed independently of all historical religions and religious bodies as a strict natural science like chemistry and astronomy 'without reference to or reliance upon any supposed exceptional or so-called miraculous revelation.'[2]

The perennial danger of such an approach is that it imposes upon theology presuppositions drawn from the world as we presently understand it. Like natural theology, the uncritical appropriation of non-Christian ethical principles can have a distorting effect on theology. The committed Christian environmentalist (or, for that matter, feminist, Marxist, Conservative, *etc.*) thus runs the risk of remaking God in his or her own image.

[1]He endowed a series of annual lectures devoted to the exploration of natural theology.

[2]Barth, 1938, p. 3.

By contrast, the Christian approach to ethics must be by way of theology. Every aspect of life is related to the God who is the creator, redeemer and fulfiller of all things.

2. The lords of creation?

a. The special status of humankind

Following the clear lead of the Bible, Christianity has consistently maintained a belief in the special status of humankind. Human beings are the chosen bearers of the divine image within creation, specially commissioned to govern creation on God's behalf. Thus we have privileges and responsibilities which we do not share with our fellow creatures.

This teaching lies at the heart of the environmentalist objections to Christian belief. Christians are incorrigibly anthropocentric, we are told.

There is a simple rejoinder. Most secular environmentalists are every bit as anthropocentric as Christians! Every non-theistic system of ethics has an anthropocentric basis. Secular ethics insists that you cannot derive an ethical statement from a descriptive statement: you cannot get an 'ought' from an 'is'. Thus ethical statements can arise only from human acts of valuing. For a non-theist, nature can be of value only because of a human decision to value it. Furthermore, most environmentalists would accept that the human species is unique in the responsibility it bears for the state of its environment.

In contrast to the radically anthropocentric nature of secular ethics, Christianity offers the possibility of creating a theocentric ethic. By thus detaching ethics from human decisions it makes possible the development of an environmental ethic in which the worth of nature is an objective reality. However, considerable work remains to be done to overcome the anthropocentrism which has been every bit as widespread in Christian doctrine and ethics as it has been in biblical studies.

b. The image of the triune God

The biblical understanding of humankind is often summarized by the doctrine of the *imago dei*, the image of God.

This metaphor for humanity is important for theologies of nature because, although it occurs rarely in the Bible, its occurrences correlate with some of the most important passages about the non-human creation (*e.g.* Gn. 1 – 11; Rom. 8; Col. 1:15–20).

i. Human versus non-human: Traditionally, the image of God has been defined by contrast with the non-human. This is the approach assumed by Lynn White. In essence, theologians have sought out particular natural characteristics of human beings which they believed were unique to humans. Two of the most popular options in this quest were freedom and rationality. The latter was particularly popular, enabling theologians to maintain the Hellenistic concept of the essential divinity of human rationality.

However, a number of points may be made against this approach. The most obvious is the sheer difficulty of finding an aspect of being human which is genuinely unique to human beings. Rightly or wrongly, the entire weight of modern science has been thrown against the notion that human beings are unique.[1] Not only has it relativized the differences between humans and animals, but it has, through the science of ecology, stressed the very intimate network of interrelationships between human and non-human. If Christian theology is to maintain the uniqueness of the human creature, it must do so without help from secular understandings of humanity.

A second difficulty is the susceptibility of this approach to ideological misuse. It is easily turned into a justification for the exploitation of nature. Combining the natural uniqueness of human beings with a belief that everything exists for a purpose, theologians in this tradition have been quick to assume that the non-human exists solely to serve the human. Thus Aquinas could say of animals, 'it is not wrong for man to make use of them, either by killing or in any other way whatever'.[2] This approach is simply not open to a theology of nature because it presupposes that humankind stands over against the non-human. It actively encourages the alienation from nature which a theology of nature must question.

[1]Its denial of human uniqueness was one of the chief theological objections to Darwinism.

[2]Cited in Regan & Singer, 1976, p. 59.

However, from a theological perspective, the most serious difficulty with defining the image of God in opposition to the non-human is that it is inherently non-theological! As I have already indicated, it looks to secular insights rather than God's self-revelation for an account of human uniqueness. Thus it opens up yet another avenue for the penetration and distortion of Christian theology by non-Christian concepts. A theology may successfully resist the temptation to remodel its concept of God on the basis of ideas from natural theology, only to allow naturalistic understandings of human nature to do the same job.

In practice, natural theology and this approach to the image of God have often been mutually reinforcing. The result has been the falsely sharp distinction between human and non-human which is so familiar in western spirituality.

The Bible *does* affirm a distinction between human and non-human. But it is not an ontological difference: both human and non-human belong to the category of creature. Instead of contrasting human and non-human, Scripture presents human beings as creatures with a special calling, a unique role in God's economy. By focusing instead on how we differ from the non-human, traditional approaches to the concept of *imago dei* easily lose sight of our kinship with creation and our calling by God.

ii. Attending to the triune God: The fact that the image of God is an explicitly theological concept suggests an alternative approach. Instead of negating the non-human we may attend to the God whose image we are supposed to portray in creation. The image of God cannot be satisfactorily understood apart from careful theological attention to the triune God and his relationships with the world of humans and non-humans.

Personal relationships constitute the very essence of God and, therefore, must lie at the very heart of Christian theology (and, indeed, our whole way of looking at the world). It is as we exercise our capacity for personal relationships that we reflect God most clearly. The image of God in human beings may be identified with this capacity to enter into personal relationships.

But is this not still too spiritual? Does it not suggest that the personal sphere is the aspect of creation that really matters?

That the rest is still secondary?

This is certainly a danger for the contemporary personalistic approach. However, it is not an inherent weakness but rather a challenge to work out the place of the non-human with some care.[1]

The activity of the triune God in relation to creation, both human and non-human, can be of assistance here. Specifically, the immanence of the Spirit and the incarnation of the Son suggest that embodiment will be essential to the divine image.[2] The incarnation, in particular, reminds us that God gives himself to what he has created. And in this self-giving he imparts a genuine, if dependent, existence and a genuine dignity to every creature.

The Persons of the Trinity are not closed in upon themselves but open to the creature. This is clearest in the life of Jesus Christ – the paradigm of being a person-in-relation to God, other human beings and the non-human creation.

c. *Creation as a gift*

At the risk of compounding the offence which some people perceive in the concept of the image of God, such an interpretation is consistent with my earlier suggestion that we understand creation as a gift. Certainly, the act of creating a free being in the above sense is, at the same time, an act of self-giving. But, more than that, the created context in which this freedom-in-relationship is worked out is itself, by virtue of its createdness, a gift.

i. Gift versus given: This notion of the world as a gift must be clearly distinguished from the classical western scientific view of the world as a given, a self-enclosed brute fact. The contrast between the two views is clearly illustrated by comparing a suggestion of the German philosopher Heidegger, with the Genesis account of creation. For Heidegger, the place of human beings in this world was adequately summarized by the word 'thrown'. We have no control over the circumstances of our birth and little control over most of the circumstances of our life – we have been *thrown* into a threatening existence and have to make the best of it. By

[1]Martin Buber, a pioneer of philosophical personalism, insisted that personal relationships extended to the non-human (*e.g.* Buber, 1970, pp. 57–58).

[2]Moltmann, 1985, pp. 244–275.

contrast, Genesis speaks of God *placing* Adam in a garden – fatherly care rather than impersonal givenness.

The world as given places limits upon the possibilities that are open to us; it determines our existence. In contrast to this, the biblical view of the world as a gift opens up new possibilities. Understood as a gift, creation points to God as the giver. A gift never refers the recipient only to itself. Rather, in the act of giving, the giver offers himself to the recipient: 'he does not only give what is his, he commends himself'.[1]

ii. Gift and freedom: A genuine gift is unconditional; it is gratuitous. Looked at in this light, human dominion over the earth is not merely stewardship. According to Genesis 1, God places no conditions upon our use of creation (except the charge to use it to the full).

Understanding creation as God's gift is the corollary of the gift of freedom implicit in our being made in God's image. However, the freedom associated with being in the image of God is very different from the formal autonomy of Enlightenment thought. The modern concept of freedom is the negative one of absence of limits imposed by others. It presents the claims of others as a threat.

By contrast, the kind of freedom consistent with image as capacity for relationship is a relational freedom. Bonhoeffer sums it up thus, 'freedom is a relationship between two persons. Being free means "being free for the other", because the other has bound me to him. Only in relationship with the other am I free.'[2] There seems no good reason for limiting this to persons: my freedom in relation to the non-human is a function of my accepting that relationship. Paradoxically, true freedom depends on recognizing the relationships (with other human beings, with God and with the non-human) which relativize it. As the psychoanalyst Rollo May points out, creativity (the positive expression of personal freedom) actually requires limits if it is to bear fruit.[3]

iii. Receiving the gift: Finally, to understand creation as a gift entails its right reception. Such an understanding is a call for gratitude and openness to the intentions of the giver.

[1]Schmitz, 1982, p. 59. [2]Bonhoeffer, 1959, p. 35.
[3]May, 1975, pp. 112f.

There are, of course, inappropriate ways of receiving a gift: strategies for its refusal. For example, the recipient may refuse to acknowledge it as such (thus exploitation of the environment may be related to the denial of the existence and call of a creator); or, he or she may simply reject the gift itself (*e.g.* the idealism of much western theology and spirituality); or, he or she may refuse to be grateful to the giver (*e.g.* by insisting on compensating the giver: the path of religious legalism).

Neither the understanding of divine image as a capacity for personal relationships nor the notion of dominion as our response to the gift of creation imposes any ontological distinction between the human and the non-human. Contrary to Lynn White's accusations, Christian theology asserts the creaturehood of human beings. St Francis' habit of addressing animals as his brothers and sisters may have been alarmingly novel, but it expressed an orthodox insight.

d. Environmental implications of disobedience and redemption

The Bible juxtaposes the affirmation that humankind is the image of God with a text in which primordial humankind is faced with the temptation to become as gods. What is presented as a gift and a vocation in Genesis 1 is seized by force in Genesis 3.

The story of the Fall is the story of how the representative creature violates the order of creation. It speaks of the denial of creation's character as a divine gift. With that denial, human dominion takes on a radically different character. Its character as divine vocation gives way to the assertion of human autonomy and absolute lordship over the world. Genesis 4 – 11 portrays human relationships with God (Babel), with one another (Cain, Lamech) and with the environment in terms of violence.

Under the impact of human disobedience, relationships cease to be characterized by free and open mutuality. Such personal relationships give way to essentially impersonal ones in which the partner is regarded as an object rather than another subject. Under these conditions dominion can be understood only in terms of the power to manipulate in accordance with one's will. A corollary of this is the inevitable alienation of human beings from the objects of their manipulation. The cost of having the world at one's disposal is that sense of thrownness of which Heidegger spoke. Alienation and domination: each gives birth to the other in a vicious circle which circumscribes all aspects of our present existence.

It follows that the re-establishment of a proper relationship between humankind and creation depends upon the redemption of that image which has been so distorted by our age-old efforts at self-deification. Conversely, a respectful concern for the environment will be an integral part of the Christian's expression of that redemption. The fact that human disobedience dooms our efforts to be only partially successful is not an argument for doing nothing.

3. Dominion and creativity

a. Concurrence

The doctrine of concurrence (or co-operation)[1] affirms that God is active in every creaturely event as its sovereign Lord without, however, compromising the relative freedom of the creature. God respects his creation; he gives it space and time to be itself. He respects its relative freedom while remaining intimately involved in every creaturely event. Thus it may be said of every event that it is willed by God. He precedes, accompanies and succeeds it. It is an act of God.

This, of course, points directly to why so many theologians have sought to suppress the doctrine since the Enlightenment. Within the limits imposed by an Enlightenment worldview it simply is not conceivable for an event to be both the act of a free creature and an act of God. As I pointed out in chapter 6, the difficulty arises from the conflict between the Enlightenment view of freedom and the biblical one.

Concurrence has two important functions in Christian talk about the relationship between God and the world. It affirms that God does not abandon his creation to its freedom. Thus it resists the tendency to deism (which was the typical stance of the Enlightenment). At the same time, it affirms the

[1]*E.g.* Barth, 1961, pp. 90–154.

relative freedom of the creature. Thus it also resists the temptation to interpret God's sovereignty in a deterministic manner (in contrast to the hyper-Calvinist reaction to the Enlightenment). By the same token, it rules out any theology which would deny divine sovereignty by allowing the creature to limit God's activity (*e.g.* process theology).

b. Dominion

The doctrine of concurrence has important implications for a theological understanding of the relationship between humankind and nature. By respecting the freedom of humankind, God has permitted us the freedom to act in God-like ways towards the rest of his creation.

Once again, we have arrived at the doctrine of human dominion over nature. Concurrence implies that we have the freedom to exercise lordship over creation. We are God's viceroys in the world.

Does this mean that God has given the human race the right and duty to behave tyrannically towards the rest of creation? Many environmentalists would have us believe this. Christianity, they say, gives divine sanction to the rape of the earth. In their eyes, dominion is merely a polite synonym for domination.

However, as we saw in chapter 5, such a view of dominion is based on anachronistic notions of kingship. An Old Testament passage promising dominion should not be read as if it assumed a modern secular understanding of power. On the contrary, it has to be read in the light of its own understanding of power and dominion. For the ancient Israelites, kingship did not imply any absolute right or authority. Instead they put the emphasis on the responsibility of the king for his realm: the ruler existed *for* his subjects.[1]

Christian concepts of dominion also have to be read in the light of a trinitarian understanding of God and his relation to creation. This introduces two important qualifications.

First, as we have already noted, creation is a gift of divine love. And God's gift to us symbolizes his gift of being to all creatures. As such, it is not simply at humankind's disposal.

[1]This was the ideal. The reality presented by the historical books of the Old Testament is a record of defection from this ideal because of human sinfulness.

Our fellow creatures are not to be destroyed merely because they inconvenience us. On the contrary, precisely because it is a gift, the natural world demands to be treated with respect. Furthermore, since it involves recognizing nature as a divine gift, a Christian understanding of dominion entails an appropriate response to the Giver.

Second, we are called to exercise dominion as the image of God. It follows that appropriate human dominion will be modelled upon the divine sovereignty. But our God is not a tyrant who delights in crushing his subjects underfoot! On the contrary, God's lordship is characterized by a love for the (recalcitrant) creature which is manifested in self-sacrificial humble service (Mk. 10:45). It is thus more appropriate to see it in terms of stewardship and priesthood than of absolute monarchy.

c. *Freedom and creativity*

Our freedom to act in God-like ways also has implications for human creativity. It is sometimes suggested that only God is genuinely creative. Against this, the implications of concurrence suggest that we are also called to be sub-creators.[1]

The calling to be sub-creators is the basis upon which Christians may legitimately interpret and give meaning to creation through the arts. However, it does not stop there. We have been granted this freedom not only to produce creations of the imagination but to influence the physical creation in which we live. We have been called to transform the world, to beautify it further. By relating the notion that human beings are the creaturely image of God to statements about God's creative activity, the Bible suggests that the calling to be sub-creators is an integral part of our calling to be God's image in creation.

This call to a creative relationship with the environment has had a chequered career in the history of Christian spirituality. There have been periods when the church as a whole has frowned upon the arts and sciences as too worldly (indeed some sections of the Christian community still take this view). However, the call to be sub-creators was taken very seriously by the Cistercian monks who did so much to

[1]Tolkien, 1964, p. 70.

develop European agriculture in the Middle Ages (and who, it seems, selected the sites of their abbeys with an eye to natural beauty). Similarly the Puritan tradition, contrary to the largely negative picture that is painted of it, encouraged Christian involvement in technology and the sciences, believing that activities which brought men and women into close contact with nature had considerable religious potential.

The freedom to act in God-like ways is our warrant for engaging in scientific research and technological innovation. But science, on this view, is more than 'thinking God's thoughts after him'. The freedom I envisage implies that science involves the creative interpretation of nature. Similarly the freedom to pursue technological innovation involves the dangerous freedom and responsibility to alter (and manage) our environment.

Thus the sciences are affirmed by Christian environmentalism. This is in sharp contrast to the anti-scientific stance of much popular environmentalism. On the other hand, neither is it merely a legitimation of the sustainable exploitation advocated by technocentric environmentalists. Christianity recognizes that we are called to manage our environment and sees a place in that management for science and technology. However, it is not motivated by self-interest but by love for God and concern for our fellow creatures.

4. Stewardship and sustenance

a. Christian environmentalism as stewardship

The term 'stewardship' has been widely deployed in recent years to justify Christian involvement in environmental action. Indeed, it would be no exaggeration to say that it has become the dominant metaphor for the Christian understanding of dominion over nature.

However, the provenance of this metaphor has been questioned. If John Passmore is to be believed,[1] Christians have not so much discovered an unnoticed implication of the

[1]Passmore, 1980, pp. 28–32.

Christian tradition, as read this concept back into Scripture and tradition in order to make them environmentally acceptable. Looking at the history of the term, he argues that until recently it was used exclusively within the social and economic spheres. The oft-quoted passage from the seventeenth-century Chief Justice, Sir Matthew Hale,[1] is dismissed as an isolated exception. Passmore concludes that 'It is certainly a mistake, indeed, to describe as "typically Christian" the view that man's duty is to preserve the face of the earth in "beauty, usefulness and fruitfulness". One should not be in the least surprised that ecological concern is sometimes condemned as heresy.'[2]

It is certainly true that stewardship has often been used to describe the responsible use of time, money and resources. Indeed for many Christians this is the primary meaning of 'stewardship'. It is also true, as Passmore points out, that the church has often seen its role as watchdog of the morals of society in terms of stewardship. However, he is quite wrong to deny its application to the natural world. Calvin (who, according to Passmore, understood stewardship as the rule of the elect over the reprobate) had this to say on the subject:

> We possess the things which God has committed to our hands, on the condition, that being content with a frugal and moderate use of them, we should take care of what shall remain. Let him who possesses a field, so partake of its yearly fruits, that he may not suffer the ground to be injured by his negligence; but let him endeavour to hand it down to posterity as he received it, or even better cultivated. Let him so feed on its fruits, that he neither dissipates it by luxury, nor permits it to be marred or ruined by neglect. Moreover, that this economy, and this diligence, with respect to those good things which God has given us to enjoy, may flourish among us; let every one regard himself as the steward of God in

[1]'The end of man's creation was that he should be the viceroy of the great God of heaven and earth in this inferior world; his steward, *villicus* [farm manager], bailiff or farmer of this goodly farm of the lower world.' Cited by Passmore, 1980, p. 30.

[2]Passmore, 1980, p. 31.

> all things which he possesses. Then he will neither conduct himself dissolutely, nor corrupt by abuse those things which God requires to be preserved.[1]

My main reservation about 'stewardship' is that it does not exhaust what the Bible and Christian theology have to say about the relationship between human beings and the natural world. In particular, it tells us little about human freedom in relation to the non-human. The emphasis is on our duties and responsibilities rather than our rights. Paradoxically, this may have the effect of undermining environmental responsibility: a bonded servant may fulfil his duties but in a less responsible manner than a free employee. We may feel that we have discharged our duty as stewards of the environment when all we have done is adhere to a set of rules.

The strength of the metaphor lies in the way it relates the rather vague Old Testament notion of dominion to the much more concrete New Testament references to household stewards. Thus it enables the development of a much clearer picture of the relationship between human beings and the environment.

Furthermore, the relationship between human dominion and divine sovereignty which has emerged in the argument so far suggests that we may fruitfully correlate the ways in which God exercises his sovereignty with the ways in which human dominion is expressed. Thus it seems natural to look to God's sustaining activity for insights into the concept of environmental stewardship.

The main feature which emerged from the earlier discussion of sustenance in trinitarian terms was its relationship to both past and future. God's present activity of sustaining creation in being refers back to the original creation: it is the preservation of creation from dissolution into chaos. But, at the same time, it refers forwards to the consummation of all things. Similarly the concept of stewardship must be developed in two ways, stressing both its conservative aspect and its creative aspect.

[1]Calvin, *C.Gn.*, 2.15.

b. Stewardship as preservation

Klaus Bockmühl[1] draws several principles from the New Testament concept of stewardship which are relevant at this point. Imagining human beings as tenant farmers within God's creation, he suggests that we have a right of use. However, we are responsible to God for the way we exercise that right. Right of use entails a duty to maintain the land in working order. Thus, at the very minimum, stewardship means sustainable exploitation.

The New Testament also enjoins a principle of sufficiency which is relevant here. It calls upon us to be content with the satisfaction of personal needs (Lk. 12:29; 1 Tim. 6:8). This call for simplicity strongly indicates a stewardship in which use is governed by need and morality.

Another parable of stewardship (the wise steward of Mt. 24:45ff.) indicates that the concept also includes a duty to care for other members of the household. This has traditionally been interpreted in anthropocentric terms, for example, 'superfluity is there for the neighbour'.[2] However, several of the findings of chapter 5 suggest that God's household extends beyond the human. Thus Christians have a duty to care for the natural world for its own sake (quite apart from any human benefits which may accrue).

In summary, environmental stewardship understood as preservation involves respect for the integrity of the non-human creation and recognition of the interdependence of human and non-human. If you like, we are the curators of God's work of art. The vocation to conserve creation justifies the actions of Christians who make common cause with environmentalists and Green activists. It requires us to maintain the present diversity of creation against further damage and to repair the damage already done by human activities.

c. Stewardship as nurture

A more dynamic understanding of stewardship is achieved by recalling that one of the first metaphors employed by the Bible to describe our care for creation is that of gardener. Adam was placed in the garden 'to work it and take care of it'

[1]Bockmühl, 1977. [2]*Ibid.*, p. 13.

(Gn. 2:15). Gardening is more than mere maintenance, it is a creative activity.

The parable of the talents (Mt. 25:14–30) also suggests a dynamic aspect to stewardship. It is not enough to preserve what we have been given in its original state. Stewardship involves a duty to develop the land.

Christian stewardship's recognition of our freedom to engage in scientific research and technological innovation, and our responsibility to manage the environment, lays it open to the risk of repudiation by ecocentric environmentalists. However, its motivation is quite different from that of technocentrism. It does not encourage the sustainable exploitation envisaged by technocentric environmentalists. On the contrary, motivated by love for God and concern for our fellow creatures, it seeks to nurture the diversity of the world.

The difference of motivation is of tremendous practical importance. Much secular environmentalism appeals to self-interest. However, this is a notoriously fragile motivation for environmental concern. As Oliver O'Donovan points out, 'Such a philosophy offers no stable protection against the exploitation of nature by man, since he can discern nothing in the relations of things to command his respect.'[1]

The positive aspect of stewardship lies in the encouragement of diversity and novelty in creation. This will include the artistic and technological transformation of our world. Nature is our responsibility: we are called to manage it.

However, we cannot stop here. What guidelines are there for the responsible use of science, technology and art in relation to the non-human? Stewardship needs to be informed by a vision of its purpose. What is the end of our stewardship? Without such a vision, stewardship must degenerate into maintenance of the *status quo* or responsible exploitation.

5. Priesthood and consummation

As Christians, the end we will have in view while we care for creation will be the final consummation of all things. But it would be helpful to have another metaphor besides that of

[1]O'Donovan, 1986, p. 52.

stewardship to convey the eschatological thrust of Christian environmental ethics.

Christian ethics is divided between past and future orientations. On the one hand, the creation ethic and natural law traditions look to the past – to the structure of creation as it was ordained by God in the beginning. On the other hand, Kingdom ethics and liberation theologies look to the future – to a vision of God's final rule.

It seems to me that we require a way of holding those different perspectives together – a way of reconciling past and future. This may be achieved by remembering that the triune God is the one who reconciles past and future: '"I am the Alpha and the Omega," says the Lord God, "who is, and who was, and who is to come, the Almighty"' (Rev. 1:8; *cf.* 21:6).

Reconciliation is usually seen as particularly appropriate to Christ, and priesthood is the dominant metaphor used to express that reconciling activity. Thus, as the title of this section indicates, I propose to explore the notion of priesthood as a way of understanding our relationship to the natural world.

a. *Creation and the priesthood of Christ*

Clearly the starting point for examining the relevance of this metaphor to environmental ethics must be Christ's priestly activity. At its very heart lies his self-offering upon the Cross. However we conceive it, it is clear that the Bible declares this act to have reversed the curse of Genesis 3. The alienation introduced into creation by human disobedience is in the process of being overcome.

The Cross is the heart but not the sum total of Christ's priestly activity. The one who offered himself once and for all exercises an eternal priesthood which flows from that central act. He is the mediator between God and humankind.

The anthropocentricity of much theological writing means that Christ's priesthood is rarely examined except as it concerns humankind. However, Eastern Orthodox theology offers an important exception to this tendency. It recognizes that, because of the unique place of humankind, Christ's priesthood must have implications which extend to the non-human creation. John Zizioulas sums up the Orthodox position thus:

> We Christians believe that what Adam failed to do

> Christ did. We regard Christ as the embodiment or *anakephalaiosis* of all creation and, therefore, as the Man *par excellence* and the saviour of the world. We regard Him, because of this, as the true 'image of God' and we associate Him with the final fate of the world. We, therefore, believe that in the person of Christ the world possesses its Priest of Creation, the model of Man's proper relation to the natural world.[1]

There are two important aspects to this priesthood of creation. In his own person, Christ has reconciled the human and the non-human (reversing Gn. 3:17), making possible a personal approach to creation. In contrast to the alienation and fragmentation which are characteristic of fallen human attitudes to nature, a personal approach draws creation up to its own level and perceives it as an integrated whole. It opens the way for the fulfilment of creation described by Paul in Romans 8:23. Through Christ, creation is 'integrated and embodied into a unified reality'.[2]

The other aspect of this priesthood is that creation is referred back to God. It is offered up to God as his own. Christ's self-offering was not only that of the sinless human but also that of the representative creature.

b. Environmentalism and the priesthood of all believers

Like the idea of dominion, priesthood can lead easily to misconceptions. Too often in the history of the church the priest has been seen as a religious authority figure, a superior class of man, specially blessed by God and empowered to pass on forgiveness, grace and spiritual insight to ordinary folk. Such a 'trickle down' theory of priesthood is a travesty of the gospel. Sadly, however, it has been (and still is) sufficiently prevalent for environmentalists to retort that such an approach is offensively patronizing.

What then is a priest, if not a religious authority figure? The simple answer is that every Christian is a priest. We are priests because, by God's grace, we have been united with and in Jesus Christ. The New Testament clearly extends the notion of priesthood to refer not only to Christ but also to the

[1]Zizioulas, 1990, p. 5. [2]*Ibid.*

entire body of Christ (1 Pet. 2:4; Rev. 1:6; 5:10; 20:6). As priests we share in the mediatorial work of Christ. That priesthood is expressed through our witness and our prayers.

A priest is a mediator and mediation is an essential part of our human vocation to have dominion over creation. One implication of the doctrine that we have been created in God's image is that, from the beginning, the human race was called to represent him to creation and vice versa. By responsibly caring for and enjoying our environment, we re-present, we make concrete, God's loving enjoyment of his creation.

Conversely, by engaging creatively with the world and offering up our works to God we are referring creation back to God. This is not to imply that the non-human creation does not, in its own way, praise its Creator. On the contrary, the so-called creation psalms of the Old Testament make it very clear that it does.[1] As priests of creation, we are called to symbolize and express at a personal level the unity of creation in praise of God.

The idea that we are priests of creation highlights the interdependence of prayer and righteous action. Without prayer environmental stewardship is incomplete. Does this mean that we ought to pray for animals? Many western Christians are likely to dismiss this suggestion out of hand. By contrast, in answer to the question, 'What is a charitable heart?', St Isaac the Syrian said,

> It is a heart which is burning with charity for the whole of creation, for men, for the birds, for the beasts, for the demons – for all creatures. He who has such a heart cannot see or call to mind a creature without his eyes becoming filled with tears by reason of the immense compassion which seizes his heart; a heart which is softened and can no longer bear to see or learn from others of any suffering, even the smallest pain, being inflicted upon a creature. This is why such a man never ceases to pray also for the animals, for the enemies of Truth, and for those who do him evil, that they may be preserved and

[1] *E.g.* Pss. 19:1–6; 104; 148.

> purified. He will pray even for the reptiles, moved by the infinite pity which reigns in the hearts of those who are becoming united to God.[1]

To pray for the non-human is to recall that it too lies within the sphere of God's loving concern. One of the functions of prayer is to align the will of the one who prays with the will of God. By voicing our concern for the environment to God we are opening up that aspect of our life to the activity of the Holy Spirit; we are saying, in effect, 'This is what bothers me. Is my anxiety appropriate? And, if so, what do you wish me to do about it?' Our activities have to be steeped in prayer because as we pray God's response to our prayers nudges us in the direction he is wanting us to take.

However, there is more to priesthood. We live in a broken world: a world despoiled by human sinfulness and exploitation. The call to share in Christ's priestly work includes a call to work for the coming of the Kingdom in its fullness. We are the representatives of one who humbled himself to serve the interests of his creatures. Following his example, we are called to self-sacrificial service on behalf of others (including non-human others). This is the logic of Mark 10:45: that the higher voluntarily serves the lower. It is the very antithesis of sustainable exploitation.

c. *The hope of creation*

Recently I was asked 'What is your vision for the environment?' When my response failed to satisfy it became apparent that what was being asked for was a manifesto or blueprint for Christian environmentalism. One can understand the concern. Too often Christians speak in vague generalities which do not make contact with the realities of the world.

However, the desire for a blueprint can be an expression of erroneous attitudes to God and humankind. It may arise from a false view of God's sovereignty. Seeking a blueprint may be a way of evading our responsibility. If God had planned all things in detail from the beginning we would need only to refer to his detailed instructions. But such

[1]Quoted in Lossky, 1957, p. 111.

detailed instructions have not been revealed to us. We have been given the freedom to develop and the responsibility to discriminate between a wide variety of environmental strategies.

Alternatively, and more commonly, blueprint hunting may indicate a false view of human powers. There is within modern Christianity a widespread Pelagian tendency to seek to bring the Kingdom into being by our own efforts. However, we are called to work alongside Christ, *not* to supplement his work of bringing the Kingdom. Works, including environmental ones, are an expression of our faith in his work.

What is my vision? It is not a blueprint. On the contrary, it is the vision of the new Jerusalem in the closing chapters of Revelation. A vision of a city! Surely not a promising place to look for an environmental vision! But it is a city which has been reconciled with the non-human creation. We are used to thinking of cities as a new kind of desert – the antithesis of nature. The new Jerusalem is a city with God's garden at its heart.

It is an inescapably optimistic vision. Environmentalism stresses the apocalyptic implications of our exploitation of the environment. Revelation reminds us, however, that God will not suffer his creation to be marred for ever by human greed and selfishness. The Kingdom will come. Meanwhile, it is our privilege as Christians to bend all our creative powers to the anticipation of the Kingdom.

CHAPTER NINE

Christian environmentalism in practice

The previous chapters have explored the spiritual implications of environmentalism and offered a theological perspective on the environment. There remains one very important dimension to be tackled. It is not enough to defend Christianity against its environmentalist critics at a purely theoretical level. The realization that care for the environment is not merely a legitimate option for some Christians but a God-given responsibility must have practical implications. In this concluding chapter I shall explore some of the things which we can do (both as individual Christians and as church members) to encourage a more biblical attitude to nature.

1. Individuals and the environment

a. Responsible use of natural resources

Recognizing that our western way of life encourages the profligate and unjust use of resources, we might look at ways in which we might begin moving towards a simpler lifestyle. In addition to its environmental implications, awareness of (and a desire for simplicity in) our lifestyle tends to make us more conscious of the inequalities within human society locally, nationally and globally. Quite apart from these considerations, desire for simplicity has been a recurring feature of Christian spirituality. Evangelicals have become increasingly aware of this in the past decade particularly through the writings of Richard Foster and Ron Sider.[1]

Many secular publications are available to help us be more responsible in our use of natural resources. A good example is *Blueprint for a Green Planet* by John Seymour and Herbert Girardet (London: Dorling Kindersley Ltd, 1987).

i. Energy conservation: In the West we take energy for granted; we consume it at a rate unprecedented in human history. It is sometimes suggested that the energy consumption of an average suburban home is comparable with that of the very wealthiest Roman estates at the time of Christ. Every one of us has at our disposal the energy equivalent of more than a hundred human slaves! We should certainly be asking whether our use of energy is wasteful.

I can begin to reduce my personal energy waste by improving the thermal insulation of my house; reducing the temperature in rooms which are little used; taking showers rather than baths; using public transport rather than private; reducing the number and wattage of lightbulbs around the house. The Energy Efficiency Office of the Department of Energy has published a number of free booklets on domestic energy conservation (including *Heating Your Home*, *Insulating Your Home* and *The Energy Friendly Home*).

At a more subtle level, I can begin to reconsider the kinds of food I eat – factory farming and intensive cultivation of arable land are made possible by high rates of energy use. Around the home, apparently innocuous commodities may have involved very high rates of energy consumption (*e.g.* aluminium foil – the extraction of aluminium from bauxite ore is extremely energy intensive). The same is true of much of the excessive packaging in which goods today are sold.

ii. Environmentally friendly products: Do I rely on

[1]Foster, 1981; Sider, 1977. Also relevant is J. White, 1979.

products which, in their manufacture or use, have a detrimental effect on the environment? Do I choose cheap products which may have been designed to have a short life (built-in obsolescence) in preference to more expensive but longer lasting items?

There has been considerable publicity about the effect upon the ozone layer of CFCs from refrigerators and aerosols. As yet, CFC-free refrigerators are not easily obtainable but there is no excuse for the continued domestic use of aerosols containing CFCs.

Many detergents and household cleaning products constitute another major domestic source of pollution. In most cases biodegradable alternatives are available. Until relatively recently these tended to be more expensive. However, consumer demand for 'Green' products has reduced the price differential to the point where it is marginal. Today there is no good reason for not using the environmentally friendly versions.

Another obvious example is unleaded petrol. It is cheaper, does less damage to the atmosphere and most modern cars can use it. Better still, the most recent cars are being fitted with catalytic converters which significantly reduce the pollutant level of exhaust fumes.

iii. Luxuries and 'labour saving' devices: Do I balk at paying marginally more for environmentally friendly domestic products while happily paying considerable sums for luxuries? Of course, it is hard to decide what is a luxury and what is not. What was a luxury ten years ago can now be found in every other home. What is a luxury to one person may well be considered a necessity by another. It would be quite wrong for me to begin to lay down rules about simplicity of lifestyle. What we do about the luxuries in our lives is a matter for our individual consciences. However, the ideal of greater simplicity, greater detachment from the materialism of our culture, is one which we should take seriously and seek to implement in our daily lives.

I might begin by asking myself whether some new luxury or labour-saving device is actually necessary. If I decide it is not, I might then consider giving the money saved to charity or Christian work. I might think twice about replacing something which has broken down: do I really need a more sophisticated replacement? Can I, in fact, manage with a simpler model or even not replace it at all?

I might take stock of my use and non-use of my possessions from time to time: can I really justify retaining something which I have not used in the past year? Some Christians may find this a particularly appropriate discipline for Lent. Possessions which are revealed in this way to be redundant may be recycled through one of the many charity shops now in existence.

I should add that there is a difference between luxury and quality. Paying a premium for a high quality product may be good stewardship. Higher reliability and greater efficiency can mean a long-term saving both in terms of money and natural resources.

iv. Further information: The above suggestions only touch the tip of the iceberg. A wealth of further information about ways of saving energy and which products are most environmentally friendly can be obtained from *The Green Consumer Guide* by John Elkington and Julia Hailes (London: Gollancz, 1988) and *The Green Consumer's Supermarket Shopping Guide* also by Elkington and Hailes (Gollancz, 1989). Articles in *Which?* Magazine are often also helpful in this respect.

b. Respect for the non-human creation

A simpler lifestyle is a step in the right direction. But, with respect to the environment, it is only a first step. Our culture's dominant attitude to nature needs to be challenged. Advocating a simpler way of living will not necessarily do that.

Many people in our culture still share the view of the American politician who was heard to comment, 'When you've seen one tree, you've seen 'em all.' For such people the natural world is no more than a resource for more or less responsible human exploitation. At the other extreme are those religious Greens who, as we have seen, deify nature.

The theology of nature outlined in the preceding chapters suggests another way of treating nature: as a fellow creature, beloved of God and entrusted to our care. Christian theology, properly understood, encourages a respect for the natural world which will not degenerate into nature worship. Helder Camara captures precisely that balance of respect without worship when he writes of 'Sister Earth'.[1]

But what does this mean in practical terms? Most of us have so little to do with nature that the American politician's comment is more likely to strike a chord with us than any call to respect our environment.

As a corrective we need to take time to re-establish contact with our natural environment. This can be achieved in many ways, for example, gardening, keeping pets, or taking walks in parks or in the countryside. If you take the trouble to look for it, nature can be found in our towns and cities (I saw foxes far more often when I lived in suburbia than I do now that I live in rural Cambridgeshire).

Of course, such activities must be engaged in responsibly. Some garden supplies may have been obtained at the expense of the natural environment (*e.g.* limestone for rockeries may have been dug out of limestone pavements, or a peat bog may have been destroyed to supply you with peat). Not all animals make suitable pets (and an increasing number of people question the morality of pet keeping). Walks in the countryside may do more harm than good if you disturb nesting birds or damage rare plants.

A tremendous variety of books is available to help you increase your appreciation of the natural world. And, of course, there are many television broadcasts on the theme. One book which I particularly enjoy is Joseph Bharat Cornell's *Sharing Nature with Children* (Watford: Exley Publications, 1979). It is a goldmine of activities and games designed to encourage a greater appreciation of nature in children (and their parents).

c. Environmental activism

All of us can help to some extent by adjusting our way of life and by being more appreciative of God's creation. However, some may want to do more. One very effective way is to join one or more of the many environmental pressure groups now campaigning for political and social changes to encourage greater concern for the environment.

This need not involve you in the sort of non-violent direct action for which Greenpeace gets so much publicity. You may

[1]Camara, 1990.

prefer to get involved in practical conservation through one of the local groups of the British Trust for Conservation Volunteers.

There are also one or two Christian environmental organizations. The most important is Christian Ecology Link (17 Burns Gardens, Lincoln, LN2 4LJ; 0522 529643). It exists to make Christians more aware of their environmental responsibility and also to promote Christian perspectives within the wider environmental movement.

d. Creativity and the environment

As I pointed out in chapter 8, an environmentalism which contents itself with preserving the *status quo* is inadequate from a Christian perspective. We are called to be creative in our relationship with the environment.

One of the easiest ways of beginning to beautify our environment is through gardening. Our homes and their surroundings can be dramatically improved by a little creative attention to appropriate plants. This is equally true whether we live in a detached house with a large garden or on the thirteenth floor of a block of flats. I am reminded of Edith Schaeffer's description of her first garden: it was grown in an old barrel on the roof of a run-down Philadelphia apartment block. Her comments on our need for nature are a striking reminder of the positive environmental potential of evangelical Christianity.

> Human beings were made to interact with growing things, not to be born, live, and die in the midst of concrete set in the middle of polluted air! ... It seems to me that to remove all direct contact with soil, seeds, plants, trees, flowers, fruit and grain is as devastating to normal, balanced, fulfilled human growth as removing all direct contact with a home with its natural interaction among human beings of different ages.[1]

[1]E. Schaeffer, 1971, pp. 86f.

e. Awareness of God as Creator

i. Encountering God in creation: One of the chief motives behind Christian environmentalism is the recognition that, throughout the Bible, the natural world is presented as a place of encounter with God.

The world in which we live is sometimes described as sacramental. What does this mean? One of the fundamental beliefs of the Christian faith is that God is the Creator of all things. The doctrine of creation does not mean merely that God made everything. Rather it implies that all things are a part of God's self-expression: creation is God's work of art and he cares deeply for every aspect of it. It also implies that God is not limited in any way by what he has created: specifically, he has not limited himself to meeting us only through prayer and the sacraments recognized by any particular denomination. On the contrary, every part of creation has the potential to become a medium through which God can speak to us, can meet with us.

But what does it mean to speak of perceiving and encountering God in creation? How does this differ from natural theology? An analogy may be drawn from the different ways in which the Bible can be read. We may legitimately read it in a search for theological insights, for truth about God and his world. And those insights may have a vital impact on our personal spirituality, affecting the way we live, and enriching our worship. Natural theology is like that. We may also read the Bible in the hope of encountering God: this is not a search for information, but an attitude of openness to God, of waiting upon him as we read. And God may honour that openness by meeting with us through the medium of the written word. We find ourselves in his presence and the words we read may strike us with the force of revelation: as personally addressed to us by God. Encountering God in creation is like this.

It follows that there can be no techniques for encountering God in creation: we cannot coerce God to meet with us. What we can do is revise our attitudes. God is unlikely to speak to us if we are unwilling to expect that possibility. The French mathematician and theologian Blaise Pascal, concluded that man facing the cosmos without God could only say, 'The eternal silence of these infinite spaces fills me with dread.'[1] Previous generations of Christians had heard the music of the spheres. They had attended to the night sky and heard the heavens telling the glory of God. However, adherence to the new science of mechanics made it increasingly difficult for Pascal's contemporaries to attend to the heavens in that way. All they were left with was a terrifying silence.

We may begin to revise our attitude by being prepared to learn from the Christian men and women who, through the ages, have met God in creation. Their example teaches us to expect such encounters. Once we begin to expect God to meet us in this way we will find that he honours our expectation. A thunder-storm, a field of corn swaying in the breeze, a sudden skylark, sunset over water, frosty cobwebs on a winter's morning, the roughness of tree bark, any aspect of God's handiwork may become a meeting place with our Creator.

The Bible is full of examples of people meditating on the natural world and finding that it directs them towards God. For example, there is Psalm 104, or Psalm 148 (in which the psalmist sees the whole of creation as a magnificent symphony of praise directed to God). A more poignant example is that of Job: the final response to his suffering takes the form of a hymn about the glory of God in creation. Where pious rationalizations and accusations failed to satisfy, a vision of God the Creator finally succeeded. Perhaps the most striking example is that of our Lord himself. It is true that God can be encountered anywhere and yet, when Jesus wanted to be alone with his Father, he took the trouble to go off into the countryside and climb a hill.

Nor are examples of encounters with God in creation lacking in subsequent Christian history. The best known example is, of course, St Francis of Assisi. He has been proclaimed the patron saint of ecology and dismissed as a heretic. Although his life story is widely known, one or two comments on his experience of the natural world are in order.

Perhaps the most important point is that his deep respect for creation developed gradually as he sought to imitate Christ. The starting point may have been his love affair with

[1] Pascal, 1966, p. 201.

Lady Poverty: his insatiable desire to identify himself with the poorest, the lowest and the meanest. It began with his rejection of the feudal hierarchical approach to human relationships in conscious imitation of the descent of Christ (Phil. 2:6–8). Gradually this openness to the lowly extended beyond the human family. Renouncing the privileges of dominion, he came to see himself as the brother of every creature.

This was no nature mysticism: Francis did not regard nature as something divine, to be worshipped. On the contrary, by calling non-human creatures his brothers and sisters he proclaimed his belief in their equality. 'And because they are brothers and sisters, they cannot be violated, but rather must be respected.'[1] Nor was it a denial of our lordship over creation but rather a profound recognition that our lordship must reflect that of Christ. His belief in the dignity of the non-human was reflected in his behaviour: in his gentle, caring acceptance of all living creatures no matter how lowly or inconvenient. Above all, by thus humbling himself before the non-human, he began to discern their song of praise to the Creator and to join in that song. The culmination of his pilgrimage with God in creation was his marvellous 'Canticle of the Creatures'.

In the Puritan tradition too we find examples of the natural world being a medium for encountering God. Typical is the experience of Jonathan Edwards, of whom it has been said that, after his conversion, 'As he walked in his father's pasture, he read the majesty and grace of God in sky and clouds, and he heard the voice and beheld the presence of God in thunder and lightning, which formerly had sent him into a fright.'[2]

Such examples (and many others) may feed our expectation of a meeting with God in creation. Another requirement is some contact with the natural world. Wherever you live that is possible. You may meet God on a Welsh hill (with Gerard Manley Hopkins or R. S. Thomas) or in the New Forest. But you do not need to live in a national park or a place of great natural beauty for this to be a practical possibility. All that is required is a walk to your local park or a nearby piece of waste ground, time to pay attention to the life

[1]Boff, 1985, p. 35. [2]Cherry, 1980, p. 16.

that can be found there and the expectation that God will meet you. Contact with the natural world need not even require you to leave your front door. If, for some reason, you are unable to get out, the view from your window, or a plant, or a pet, or one of the many excellent natural history programmes broadcast by the BBC or ITV will suffice.

Seeking to meet God in this way is by no means a passive exercise. On the contrary, it is every bit as active as the discipline of reading Scripture in the expectation of meeting God through its pages.

ii. Praising the Creator: Christianity claims that all things are part of God's good creation, the natural world is good in itself and all this beauty has been entrusted to our care as a gift of divine love. No wonder it has been called the most materialistic of religions! Sadly, we have not always responded in an appropriate way. Nevertheless, that affirmation of the goodness of creation is so fundamental to our faith that it is embedded in the very heart of the eucharist. Furthermore, it may well-up at the most unlikely times. For example, during a service to mark the end of the 1905 Lincoln typhoid epidemic, Bishop Edward King was able to say,

> I will thank Him for the pleasures given me through my senses, for the glory of the thunder, for the mystery of music, the singing of birds and the laughter of children. I will thank Him for the pleasures of seeing, for the delights through colour, for the awe of the sunset, the beauty of flowers, the smile of friendship and the look of love; for the changing beauty of the clouds, for the wild roses in the hedges, for the form and the beauty of birds, for the leaves on the trees in spring and autumn, for the witness of the leafless trees through the winter, teaching us that death is sleep and not destruction, for the sweetness of flowers and the scent of hay. Truly, O Lord, the earth is full of thy riches![1]

Jesus taught that 'Man shall not live by bread alone.' Christianity also affirms that neither shall he live by blessings

[1]Quoted in Newton, 1977, p. 113.

alone. Recognizing our dependence upon a world which God has given into our care points us back to the God who is the ultimate provider. The appropriate response is thanksgiving. However, as the above quotation makes clear, such thanksgiving goes far beyond such recognition of dependence. It covers also the sheer gratuity of natural beauty.

iii. A praise walk: Here are a few practical suggestions for beginning to find God in creation for yourself. This may be done in the context of a short walk. It will be a time of prayer but, instead of bowing your head, shutting your eyes and seeking God within, it will demand that you use all your senses as much as possible.

Since it is a time of prayer, begin by taking a few moments to relax and become aware of God's presence and his love for you.

As you step outside, breathe deeply . . . reflect on how you take the air you breathe for granted. Think about the other necessities of life which God provides.

When you have walked far enough to be out of earshot of anyone, pause and make conscious, prayerful use of each one of your senses in turn.

Sight: Use your vision to revel in, enjoy, discern the colour, shape, texture, depth, movement of everything around you. Think about what the beauty you see contributes to your life. Consider the privilege and responsibility which God has given you in the gift of all this beauty. Express to God your thanksgiving and praise.

Hearing: Stop for a while and really listen, listen to the silence which, in reality, abounds with natural sounds. Listen for the breeze blowing through the trees or through the long grass; listen for the song of birds and for the hum of insects. Imagine the wind, the trees, the insects and the birds all blending their voices together in a song of praise to their Creator. Add your voice to their worship.

Touch: Become conscious of the feeling of the sun and the air on your skin, the textures of clothing, trees, grass, stones, the sensation of the ground through your shoes.

If you have time, you might like to do the same with your senses of taste and smell.

Conclude by finding one thing which summarizes for you what you have experienced during this walk.

It is possible to do something of this sort whether you live in the depths of the countryside or in the heart of a big city. You may have to relax what I said about being alone, but apart from that there is no reason why you shouldn't go for a praise walk around any city park.

But what about the intrusion of 'civilization'? As you breathe deeply at the beginning of the walk you may choke on exhaust fumes from a passing motor car. Is it practical to attempt to develop this kind of attitude to nature in an urban environment? If you have lived in the British countryside for any length of time, you will realize that none of it is untouched by human hand. The quiet of the countryside near my home is regularly shattered by the sound of military jets from nearby airforce bases, and every autumn the area is enveloped in shrouds of smoke as the local farmers burn the stubble in their fields.

Wherever you attempt this walk of praise you are likely to come across evidence of our exploitation of nature. Thus your walk may also become a walk of repentance, sensitizing you to the ways in which we mar our environment.

As you engage in this sort of activity, you are likely to find that it begins to have an impact on the rest of your life. The priestly stewardship which I outlined earlier may be the appropriate attitude with which to begin to perceive God in creation. It is equally true that as you begin to look for God in creation your attitude to nature will change.

2. Churches and the environment

a. Awareness of God as Creator

All mainline churches at least pay lipservice to the doctrine of creation. However, apart from regular recitation of the First Article of the Creed, expression of that commitment may be minimal. In some denominations, creation may appear as a theme for Sunday worship as little as once a year: and that may be a service which is often dismissed by committed Christians as a semi-pagan gesture to folk religion, namely, the Harvest Festival.

The Harvest Festival is an obvious starting point for

greater emphasis on creation within Christian life and worship. Indeed, it has already been used by such organizations as the Worldwide Fund of Nature as a focal point for reflection on the religious dimensions of environmentalism. Unfortunately the value of that material for general Christian worship is undermined by its multi-faith nature. There is considerable scope for considering our call to be stewards of creation in the context of such a service.

The modern Harvest Festival dates back to 1843, when the vicar of Morwenstow in Cornwall held a communion service using bread made from the new corn of that year's harvest. It recalls the old festival of Lammas (*Llaf-maesse* or loaf mass) which was an English Christian festival of first-fruits (based on Dt. 26:1–11).

But Harvest Festivals are only the beginning. More emphasis could be placed upon the implications of major doctrines for our attitude to nature. Similarly, the sacraments have a role to play, for example, one dimension of the Eucharist which has been lost in western theologies is that of its sanctification of the material creation. We are too quick to spiritualize our worship and overlook the fact that it is through the material creation (water, wine and bread) that God communicates his presence.

b. Respect for the non-human creation

As church members we can encourage one another to take a more positive attitude to nature. This could very well begin with our use of church property. In Britain the churches still own significant tracts of land. How are we using that land? Do we treat it as an inconvenience to be dealt with as cost-effectively as possible (*e.g.* covered in concrete and treated regularly with weedkiller)? Is it regarded purely as a source of income?

Our contribution to conservation and environmentalism could begin with church property. This could be on a small scale, such as turning the churchyard into a conservation area. In fact, church property is often an unintentional conservation area! Many urban and suburban churchyards and vicarage gardens have become oases of nature in deserts of bricks and concrete. In rural areas the churchyard may be a haven for meadow plants which, since the advent of industrial farming, have become increasingly rare. On a more ambitious scale, congregations may turn a critical eye on the environmental activities of their denomination (*e.g.* lobbying for the environmentally responsible use of glebe land) or encourage greater environmental sensitivity within the local community.

c. Responsible use of natural resources

The local church could also play a role in encouraging its members to adopt a simpler lifestyle. One suggestion which has often been made but, sadly, less often taken up is that of a church equipment-pool. The church could encourage the sharing of tools, sports equipment, books, items of furniture and even cars. Anything which a family might want to use, but not with sufficient frequency to justify owning one, could be pooled by the church.

The principle of responsible stewardship certainly applies to the church's own plant and equipment. For example, most churches in the U.K. use a great deal of paper for newsletters and service sheets. Is all of this really necessary? And, when we have cut out the unnecessary uses of paper, what is our excuse for not using recycled paper for the rest?

Energy conservation is clearly an issue for congregations forced to use historic but draughty buildings. The Church of Scotland has done a good deal of work on energy conservation in church buildings and this has been summarized in two booklets: *Make the Most Of It* (1980) and *Make Even More Of It* (1986) (both available from the General Trustees of the Church of Scotland, 121 George St, Edinburgh, EH2 4YR).

Is your church building an asset to the local environment or an eyesore? Francis Schaeffer highlighted this question with an account of a visit to a pagan community near a Christian college at which he had been lecturing:

> It was then that I realized what a horrible situation this was. When I stood on Christian ground and looked at the Bohemian people's place, it was beautiful. They had even gone to the trouble of running their electricity cables under the level of the trees so that they couldn't be seen. Then I stood on pagan ground and looked at the Christian community and

> saw ugliness. That is horrible. Here you have a Christianity that is failing to take into account man's responsibility and proper relationship to nature.[1]

Surrounding a new church building with asphalt may be easy to maintain and useful for parking. But what does it do for the environment? Trees and shrubs need not be very costly and may greatly enhance the environment.

Francis Schaeffer used to say that the church is a pilot plant for the Kingdom of God. That holds true for our relationship with the environment. As individuals and as believing communities we should be demonstrating the implications of redemption for our relationship with the natural world.

[1] F. Schaeffer, 1970, p. 42.

Bibliography

A note on the references

In most cases I have adopted the author–date system. This does not apply to the works of classical authors which appear in many different editions. In these cases I have referred to them by title and the traditional textual divisions. The reference below is to the edition I have used in preparing this volume.

Abbreviations

The following abbreviations occur in the footnotes and references:

NDCT *A New Dictionary of Christian Theology*, ed. A. Richardson & J. Bowden (London: SCM, 1983).

NDT *New Dictionary of Theology*, ed. S. B. Ferguson & D. F. Wright (Leicester & Downers Grove, Ill.: IVP, 1988).

SJT *Scottish Journal of Theology*.

SS *The Study of Spirituality*, ed. C. Jones, G. Wainwright & E. Yarnold (London: SPCK, 1986).

Works cited

Augustine, *Conf.*, *Confessions*, Harmondsworth: Penguin, 1961.
—, *Trin.*, *The Trinity*, The Fathers of the Church, Volume 45, Washington D.C.: Catholic University of America Press, 1963.
—, *Ver.*, 'Of True Religion', in *Augustine: Earlier Writings*, tr. J. Burleigh, London, 1953, pp. 225–283.

Barbour, I. G., 1990, *Religion in an Age of Science*, London: SCM.
Barr, J., 1972, 'Man and Nature – The Ecological Controversy and the Old Testament', *Bulletin of John Rylands Library*, 55, pp. 9–32.
Barrow, J. D., & Tipler, F. J., 1986, *The Anthropic Cosmological Principle*, Oxford: Clarendon Press.
Barth, K., 1938, *The Knowledge and the Service of God According to the Teaching of the Reformation*, London: Hodder & Stoughton.
—, 1961, *Church Dogmatics, Vol 3: The Doctrine of Creation, Part 3*, Edinburgh: T. & T. Clark.
Bavel, T. van, 1963, *Répertoire Bibliographique de Saint Augustin, 1950–1960*, The Hague: Nijhoff.
Berkouwer, G. C., 1952, *The Providence of God*, Grand Rapids, Mich.: Eerdmans.
Blackmore, V., & Page, A., 1989, *Evolution: The Great Debate*, Oxford: Lion.
Blackstone, W. T., 1974, 'Ethics and Ecology', *Philosophy and the Environmental Crisis*, ed. W. T. Blackstone, Athens, Geo.: University of Georgia Press, pp. 16–42.
Blocher, H., 1984, *In The Beginning: The Opening Chapters of Genesis*, Leicester: IVP.
Bockmühl, K., 1977, *Conservation and Lifestyle*, Nottingham: Grove Books.
Boff, L., 1985, *Saint Francis: A model for human liberation*, London: SCM.
Bonhoeffer, D., 1959, *Creation and Fall: A Theological Interpretation of Genesis 1 – 3*, London: SCM.
Brueggeman, W., 1982, *Genesis*, Atlanta, Geo.: John Knox Press.

Buber, M., 1970, *I and Thou*, tr. W. Kaufman, Edinburgh: T. & T. Clark.

Calvin, J., *C.Gn.*, *Commentaries on the First Book of Moses, called Genesis*, tr. J. King, Edinburgh: Calvin Translation Society, 1848.

—, *C. Jn.*, *Commentary on the Gospel According to John*, tr. W., Pringle, Edinburgh: Calvin Translation Society, 1847.

—, *Inst.*, *Institutes of the Christian Religion* (1559 edition), tr. F. L. Battles, Library of Christian Classics, Vols. 20 – 21, Philadelphia: Westminster Press, 1960.

—, *Praed.*, *Concerning the Eternal Predestination of God*, tr. J. K. S. Reid, London: James Clarke & Co., 1961.

Camara, H., 1990, *Sister Earth: Ecology & the Spirit*, London: New City.

Cherry, C., 1980, *Nature and Religious Imagination. From Edwards to Bushnell*, Philadelphia: Fortress.

Cranfield, C. E. B., 1974, 'Some Observations on Romans 8. 19–21', *Reconciliation and Hope (The Leon Morris Festschrift)*, ed. R. Banks, Exeter: Paternoster.

—, 1975, *A Critical and Exegetical Commentary on the Epistle to the Romans, Vol. 1: Introduction and Commentary on Romans I-VIII*, International Critical Commentary, Edinburgh: T. & T. Clark.

Cumbey, C., 1983, *The Hidden Dangers of the Rainbow: The New Age and our Coming Age of Barbarism*, Shreveport: Huntington House.

Cupitt, D., 1983, *Creation out of Nothing*, London: SCM.

Darwin, C., 1928, *The Origin of Species*, Everyman's Library No. 811, London: Dent.

Devall, B., & Sessions, G., 1985, *Deep Ecology: Living as if nature mattered*, Salt Lake City: Peregrine Smith Books.

Dumbrell, W. J., 1984, *Covenant and Creation: An Old Testament Covenantal Theology*, Exeter: Paternoster.

Edwards, J., 1971, 'Observations Concerning the Trinity and the Covenant of Redemption', *Treatise on Grace and other posthumously published writings by Jonathan Edwards*, ed. P. Helm, London: J. Clarke & Co.

Faricy, R., 1987, 'The Person–Nature Split: Ecology, Women, and Human Life', *Irish Theological Quarterly*, 53, pp. 203–218.

Ferguson, M., 1981, *The Aquarian Conspiracy: Personal & social transformation in the 1980s*, London: RKP.

Foster, R., 1981, *Freedom of Simplicity*, London: Triangle.

Fox, M., 1981, *Whee! We, Wee All the Way Home: A guide to sensual, prophetic spirituality*, Santa Fe, NM: Bear & Co.

—, 1983, *Original Blessing: A Primer in Creation Spirituality*, Santa Fe, NM: Bear & Co.

Funkenstein, A., 1986, *Theology and the Scientific Imagination: from the Middle Ages to the Seventeenth Century*, Princeton, NJ: Princeton University Press.

Gilkey, L., 1976, *Reaping the Whirlwind: A Christian Interpretation of History*, New York: Seabury.

Gowan, D. E., 1987, *Eschatology in the Old Testament*, Edinburgh: T. & T. Clark.

Gregory of Nyssa, *Abl.*, 'An Answer to Ablabius: That We Should not Think of Saying There Are Three Gods', *Christology of the Later Fathers*, ed. E. R. Hardy, Philadelphia: Fortress, 1954, pp. 256–267.

Hankey, W., 1987, *God in Himself: Aquinas' Doctrine of God as Expounded in the Summa Theologiae*, Oxford: Oxford University Press.

Hardin, G., 1972, *Exploring New Ethics for Survival: The Voyage of the Spaceship Beagle*, New York: Viking Books.

Hardy, D. W., & Ford, D. F., 1984, *Jubilate: Theology in Praise*, London: DLT.

Heim, K., 1935, *God Transcendent: Foundation for a Christian Metaphysic*, London: Nisbet & Co.

Hendry, G. S., 1980, *Theology of Nature*, Philadelphia: Westminster.

Hooykaas, R., 1972, *Religion and the Rise of Modern Science*, Edinburgh: Scottish Academic Press.

Jenson, R. W., 1973, *Story and Promise: A Brief Theology of the Gospel about Jesus*, Philadelphia: Fortress.

—, 1982a, 'Creation as a Triune Act', *Word & World*, 2, pp. 34–42.

—, 1982b, *The Triune Identity: God According to the Gospel*, Philadelphia: Fortress.
Josipovici, G., 1988, *The Book of God: A response to the Bible*, New Haven & London: Yale University Press.
Jüngel, E., 1976, *The Doctrine of the Trinity: God's Being is in Becoming*, Edinburgh: Scottish Academic Press.

Kaiser, C. B., 1991, *Creation and the History of Science*, History of Christian Theology, Vol. 3, London: Marshall Pickering.
Kaufman, G., 1981, *The Theological Imagination: Constructing the Concept of God*, Philadelphia: Fortress.
Kidner, D., 1975, *Psalms 73 – 150: A Commentary on Books III – V of the Psalms*, Tyndale OT Commentary 14b, London: IVP.

Langford, M. J., 1981, *Providence*, SCM.
Lossky, V., 1957, *The Mystical Theology of the Eastern Church*, Cambridge & London: J. Clarke & Co.
Lovejoy, A. O., 1936, *The Great Chain of Being: A Study of the History of an Idea*, Cambridge, Mass.: Harvard University Press.
Lovejoy, A., O., & Boas, G., 1935, *Primitivism and Related Ideas in Antiquity*, Baltimore: John Hopkins Press.
Lovelock, J. E., 1979, *Gaia: A new look at life on Earth*, Oxford: Oxford University Press.
—, 1988, *The Ages of Gaia: A biography of our living Earth*, Oxford: Oxford University Press.

May, R., 1975, *The Courage to Create*, New York: W. W. Norton.
Meyendorff, J., 1983, 'Creation in the History of Orthodox Theology', *St Vladimir Theological Quarterly*, 27, pp. 27–37.
Moltmann, J., 1985, *God in Creation: An Ecological Doctrine of Creation*, London: SCM.
Mooney, C., 1968, *Teilhard de Chardin and the Mystery of Christ*, Garden City, NY: Doubleday & Co.

Newton, J. A., 1977, *Search for a Saint: Edward King*, London: Epworth.

O'Connell, R. J., 1978, *Art and the Christian Intelligence in St Augustine*, Oxford: Blackwell.

O'Donnell, J. J., 1983, *Trinity and Temporality: The Christian Doctrine of God in the Light of Process Theology and the Theology of Hope*, Oxford: Oxford University Press.

O'Donovan, O., 1986, *Resurrection and Moral Order: An Outline for Evangelical Ethics*, Leicester: IVP.

O'Riordan, T., 1981, *Environmentalism*, 'Research in Planning and Design', Vol. 2, ed. A. J. Scott, revised edition, London: Pion.

Ogden, S., 1977, *The Reality of God*, New York: Harper & Row.

Pannenberg, W., 1968, *Jesus – God and Man*, London: SCM.

Pascal, B., 1966, *Pensées*, Harmondsworth: Penguin.

Passmore, J., 1980, *Man's Responsibility for Nature: Ecological Problems and Western Traditions*, London: Duckworth.

Peacocke, A. R., 1979, *Creation and the World of Science*, Oxford: Oxford University Press.

Pedler, K., 1979, *The Quest for Gaia: A Book of Changes*, London: Souvenir Press.

Pittenger, N., 1968, *Process Thought and Christian Faith*, Welwyn: J. Nisbet & Co.

Porritt, J., 1984, *Seeing Green: The Politics of Ecology Explained*, Oxford: Blackwell.

Porritt, J., & Winner, D., 1988, *The Coming of the Greens*, London: Collins.

Rahner, K., 1970, *The Trinity*, tr. J. Donceel, Tunbridge Wells: Burns & Oates.

Regan, T., & Singer, P. (eds.), 1976, *Animal Rights and Human Obligations*, New Jersey: Prentice-Hall.

Regenstein, L. G., 1991, *Replenish the Earth: A History of Organized Religion's Treatment of Animals and Nature*, London: SCM.

Reumann, J., 1973, *Creation and New Creation: The Past, Present, and Future of God's Creative Activity*, Minneapolis: Augsburg.

Russell, C., 1985, *Cross-Currents: Interactions Between Science & Faith*, Leicester: IVP.

Russell, P., 1982, *The Awakening Earth: Our Next Evolutionary Leap*, London: RKP.

Santmire, H. P., 1980, 'St. Augustine's Theology of the Biophysical World', *Dialog*, 19, 174–185.

—, 1985, *The Travail of Nature: The Ambiguous Ecological Promise of Christian Theology*, Philadelphia: Fortress.
Schaeffer, E., 1971, *Hidden Art*, London: Norfolk Press.
Schaeffer, F., 1970, *Pollution and the Death of Man: The Christian View of Ecology*, Wheaton, Ill.: Tyndale House.
—, 1973, *Art and the Bible*, London: Hodder & Stoughton.
Schall, J., 1971, 'Ecology – an American Heresy?', *America*, 124.
Schmitz, K., 1982, *The Gift: Creation*, Milwaukee: Marquette University Press.
Sider, R., 1977, *Rich Christians in an Age of Hunger*, London: Hodder & Stoughton.
Smail, T., 1988, *The Giving Gift: The Holy Spirit in Person*, London: Hodder & Stoughton.
Spretnak, C., 1986, *The Spiritual Dimension of Green Politics*, Santa Fe, NM: Bear & Co.
Starhawk, 1979, *The Spiral Dance: A Rebirth of the Ancient Religion of the Great Goddess*, San Francisco: Harper & Row.
Steck, O. H., 1980, *World and Environment*, Biblical Encounter Series, Nashville, Tenn.
Steiner, S., 1976, *The Vanishing White Man*, New York: Harper & Row.

Tanner, K., 1988, *God and Creation in Christian Theology*, Oxford: Blackwell.
Teilhard de Chardin, P., 1965, *The Phenomenon of Man*, tr. B. Wall, London: Collins.
—, 1974, *Let Me Explain*, London: Collins.
Thunberg, L., 1965, *Microcosm and Mediator: The Theological Anthropology of Maximus the Confessor*, Acta seminarii Neotestamentici Upsaliensis XXV, Lund.
Tolkien, J. R. R., 1964, 'On Fairy Stories', *Tree and Leaf*, London: Allen & Unwin, pp. 11–79.

Waddell, H., 1934, *Beasts and Saints*, London: Constable & Co.
Weber, O., 1981, *Foundations of Dogmatics: Volume 1*, tr. D. L. Guder, Grand Rapids, Mich.: Eerdmans.
Westcott, B. F., 1890, 'The Incarnation and Nature', *Christus Consummator: Some Aspects of the Work and Person of Christ in Relation to Modern Thought*, London, pp. 131–143.

Westermann, C., 1974, *Creation*, London: SPCK.
—, 1984, *Genesis 1 – 11: A Commentary*, London: SPCK.
White, J., 1979, *The Golden Cow: Materialism in the Twentieth-Century Church*, London: Marshall, Morgan & Scott.
White, L. Jr., 1967, 'The Historical Roots of our Ecologic Crisis', *Science*, 155, pp. 1203–1207.
—, 1968, *Machina Ex Deo: Essays in the Dynamism of Western Culture*, Cambridge, Mass.: MIT Press.
—, 1973, 'Continuing the Conversation', *Western Man and Environmental Ethics*, ed. I. G. Barbour, Reading, Mass.: Addison-Wesley, pp. 55–64.
Whitehead, A. N., 1979, *Process and Reality*, New York: The Free Press.
Wilkinson, L. (ed.), 1980, *Earthkeeping: Christian Stewardship of Natural Resources*, Grand Rapids, Mich.: Eerdmans.

Yi-Fu, T., 1970, 'Our Treatment of the Environment in Ideal and Actuality', *American Scientist*, 58, pp. 244–249.
Young, N., 1976, *Creator, Creation and Faith*, London: SCM.

Zimmerli, W., 1964, 'The Place and Limit of Wisdom in the Framework of Old Testament Theology', *SJT*, 17, pp. 146–158.
Zizioulas, J. D., 1985, *Being As Communion: Studies in Personhood and the Church*, London: DLT.
—, 1990, 'Preserving God's Creation: Three lectures on Theology and Ecology', III, *King's Theological Review*, 13, pp. 1–5.